THE FORCE:

DAVID ROBINSON,
THE NBA'S
NEWEST SKY-HIGH
SENSATION

ALSO BY JIM SAVAGE

The Encyclopedia of the NCAA Basketball
Tournament

The 1991 Yearbook of the NCAA Basketball
Tournament

THE FORCE:

DAVID ROBINSON,
THE NBA'S NEWEST SKY-HIGH SENSATION

JIM SAVAGE

A DELL BOOK

Published by
Dell Publishing
a division of
Bantam Doubleday Dell Publishing Group, Inc.
666 Fifth Avenue
New York, New York 10103

ISBN: 0-440-21227-8

Printed in the United States of America

Published simultaneously in Canada

April 1992

10   9   8   7   6   5   4   3   2   1

OPM

For my mother

CONTENTS

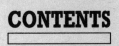

"I searched very hard to find that one thing I could be great at, and suddenly I found myself seven feet tall. I guess it better be basketball."

—*David Robinson*

PROLOGUE

THE FORCE

Of the major team sports, only basketball lets us see evolution take place before our eyes.

In baseball, things are eternal. Rickie Henderson takes off at the crack of the bat and takes out the second sacker to keep him from completing the double play. Just like Jackie Robinson, or Ty Cobb. Football too remains much the same as it's been for decades. The players are bigger and faster than they were a generation ago, but interior linemen still push would-be tacklers off the line, and linebackers still fight through the blocks to get to the ball carrier. The same way they did when Vince Lombardi's Green Bay Packers ruled the NFL.

The fundamentals of football and baseball have not changed in a generation.

But in basketball, the way the game is played changes every time a great player steps on the court:

Thirty-five years ago, Big Bill Russell redefined the role of the center. With the speed of a small man and uncanny leaping ability and timing, he blocked shots, grabbed rebounds and, as the most intimidat-

1

ing defensive player in history, turned an average Boston Celtics team into a dynasty. He made defense matter.

When Wilt "The Stilt" Chamberlain broke into the NBA, his agility, skill, and power reinvented the offensive role of the pivotman. A great rebounder and a scoring machine, with a money-in-the-bank fallaway jumper that enabled him to *average* 50 points a game, he was the man to "go to" for 2 points.

A decade later, Kareem Abdul-Jabbar brought a new package of skills to the center position, including his sky hook, the most unstoppable shot ever. But along with his scoring, rebounding, and defensive prowess, the vision of his 7-2 frame dribbling downcourt brought gasps from spectators who had never seen a big man put the ball on the floor before. No one had ever thought that a man his size could have such refined two-way skills. He was the model on whom all future centers would be judged.

From another, more compact, perspective, Oscar Robertson was the whole package. He was a new type of point guard, bigger and stronger than the rest. He could shoot, pass, post up, dribble the ball as if it were on a string, and break the press better than anybody. One year Oscar *averaged* a triple-double. Despite his size, athletic ability, and superb stats, the Big O never dunked; he simply didn't believe in it.

Five years after the Big O retired, Magic Johnson and Larry Bird came into the league. Like Robertson before them, they gave new meaning to the words team player. Magic, a 6-9 point guard, and Bird, a 6-9 point forward, each displayed an unparalleled ability to see the court and hit the open man. Their greatness raised the level of everyone around them, and their names have become indelibly linked as the two great champions of the eighties.

On another plane, Connie Hawkins—the Hawk —took off from the hard asphalt playgrounds of Bedford-Stuyvesant, and cradling a basketball in one massive hand like it was a grapefruit, soared and stuffed and carried the game into a new, above-the-rim dimension. Doctor J took the Hawk one step farther, rising even higher with an artist's vision and a dancer's grace. And Michael Jordan, of course, simply defies gravity as no player has ever done before.

Each one, in his own time, has defined the state of the art of basketball. And each of the game's greatest players has carried his team to new heights, turning losers into contenders and competitors into champions.

Which brings us to the present—and to David Robinson. No one has ever more completely redefined his position. And no one has ever done more to turn a squad around than the Spurs' superstar center.

□

Standing ramrod straight like the Naval officer he is, David is 7′1″ tall, and yet he runs the floor faster than the quickest small forwards. His legs are thin and long and sinewy, and while his chest tapers down to a 33-inch waist, his biceps are gigantic and his muscles well defined. He weighs 235 pounds, but he dominates bigger, bulkier men in the paint. He has the quick reflexes and analytical ability of a point guard, and his coach, Larry Brown, marvels, "I've seen this kid dribble the length of the floor as if he were a guard. We take it for granted, because sometimes when you're watching him he looks like he's six feet tall.''

While Michael soars on his jump, David explodes. His dunks are swift and certain, and his ability to spring instantaneously off the floor—to leap for a block or a rebound, come back down and immediately lift off again—is without parallel in basketball history.

And what terrifies opponents the most is that the ex-Navy man is still just learning the game.

□

There's no question David Robinson plays basketball like nobody else on earth. On the court, he's an almost unearthly combination of size, speed, grace, and intelligence. Quicker than any man his size has ever been and with tremendous leaping ability, he is an awesome shot-blocker. And once he rejects the shot —often controlling the ball by tapping it over to a teammate—he takes off downcourt, flying across on the wing to rematerialize and finish the fast break he started with a lightning left-handed dunk.

Mr. Robinson's neighborhood is in the stratosphere, a place where very few others have ever gone. He is becoming one of those rare players who single-handedly changes the way the game of basketball is played. Earvin Johnson is Magic . . . Michael Jordan is Air . . . and David Robinson is *The Force*.

But who is the man behind the dunks? And where did he come from?

CHAPTER I

THE PLEBE

By eight o'clock in the morning on July 6th, 1983, the midshipmen on watch had already waved most of the incoming class of 1,356 plebes through the gates of the Naval Academy. Many had arrived the day before, and the others, who lived close enough to Annapolis to drive into the sleepy seaside town that morning, were quickly being pointed in the right direction. Those familiar with Maryland summers were thankful that it would not be too hot a day, and that the breeze off the Severn River would keep things comfortable. The handsome, fresh-faced young black man uncurled his long legs out of his parents' car, raised himself to his full height, and said good-bye to his father. He surveyed his new surroundings. He was a plebe at the Naval Academy—a freshman—and he knew, as all college freshmen know when they leave for school, that his life would never be the same again.

Midshipman-to-be David Robinson might have taken a moment to look out at the harbor, to catch a quick glimpse of a sloop sailing beyond the protected inlet toward Chesapeake Bay and from there to the open sea. Sometime during the day he most certainly walked past the statue of Tecumseh, and he may have even saluted the stern Indian warrior who watched over the corps of midshipmen under his care. He probably took note of the large Gothic chapel, and might have imagined it on a Sunday morning, filled with middies in their white dress uniforms. He surely stood at the base of the massive Rotunda, gazing up at the portraits and mementos of Navy tradition that lined the walls.

But David wasn't there to sightsee—his day was taken up with work. Along with his classmates, he stood on endless lines, answering questions, filling out forms, listening to instructions. He registered for classes, equipment, housing, and military training. And like most of his fellow plebes, an odd combination of conflicting emotions—excitement, apprehension, happiness, curiosity, and more—almost certainly raced through his mind.

At just over 6-8 (he had grown an inch since his acceptance into the Academy) David towered over his new classmates. Two years earlier, when he'd first started thinking about an appointment, he was just 6-4 and a high school junior. But then he'd shot up beyond the Navy's 6-6 height limit, and along with a limited number of other plebes needed a waiver to be admitted. Now he was even taller than the waiver limit of 6-8. But Navy didn't go back on its word: since he'd already been promised a place in the class of '87, he was a midshipman for as long as he could hack it.

Looking around over the heads of his fellow

plebes, Midshipman Robinson had to be deeply aware of just how different he was from most of them. The Academy was in the midst of a major push to recruit more African-American and other non-white students, and Navy had also begun to accept women into the ranks. Still he couldn't help but notice that fewer than 10 percent of his classmates were minority students. But David was used to living among white people. His parents, themselves victims of racism as children in the segregated South, had tried to ensure that their children would not suffer from the same sort of second-class citizenship by choosing always to live in integrated areas. And besides, David knew that the Academy's policy on racism was crystal clear: anybody who showed even the slightest trace of overt prejudice in his relations with fellow midshipmen would be booted out faster than a seaman is required to salute an admiral.

Like every plebe David spent a good part of Induction Day (when new arrivals at the Naval Academy register for duty), questioning whether Navy was really the right place for him. There were lots of good reasons why he chose to go—reasons that led him to trade in his jeans that morning for the spit and polish dress uniform of a midshipman. His parents had always stressed the value of education, and he knew that in his field—engineering and mathematics—there were few schools that compared with Navy. That's why, even as a junior in high school down in Virginia Beach, he had thought about going to Annapolis. He understood that while a top-quality college would not be cheap, if he qualified for the Academy, it would be *free.* He'd get an excellent education and a prestigious degree—all he had to do was work hard and maintain discipline.

When it was over, David also knew he'd have to serve five years as a Naval officer. But that didn't scare him either—his father Ambrose had been a chief petty officer and a sonar technician in the Navy for twenty years—so he was hardly a stranger to the military way of life.

All day long David endured the endless lines and looked forward to the ceremony that would cap I Day, when he would join his fellow plebes and be sworn into the Academy. Finally, the moment came: David Robinson was officially a midshipman.

He never expected what came next. After the plebes took the oath of induction, they were ushered back to the seemingly limitless expanse of Bancroft Hall—"Mother B"—where every single one of them would eat, sleep, and report for duty for as long as they remained at the Academy. Years later David would recall that suddenly the upperclassmen and officers "started yelling at us and telling us where to go. Most of the day they were pretty polite, but then they weren't polite at all. I remember thinking, 'What have I gotten myself into?'"

☐

Plebe Summer is about total immersion and transformation. Each year it instantly turns fresh-faced high school grads into disciplined midshipmen. And like almost everything else at the Naval Academy, it's a tradition.

As a young Marine officer and recent graduate of the Academy remarked, "Plebes have a lot to learn."

For David Robinson, who arrived in the yard an easygoing, friendly, and not yet eighteen-year-old boy, the lessons started right away. David's Plebe Summer was an endless round of military training punctuated by the constant reinforcement of the code of discipline and honor by which every Naval officer is expected to live. The campus atmosphere—despite the manicured beauty and appearance of refined gentility—was that of a boot camp.

At five o'clock each morning reveille jarred the plebes out of their beds. A half hour later, they fell in for morning formation. Their shoes were shined—perfectly polished to reflect light—and their uniforms pressed to a T. For the next seventeen hours they learned how to march, how to salute, how to use weapons, how to stand watch, how to think, act, and breathe—the Navy way.

The Plebe Summer conditioning regimen—from pushups to running to obstacle courses to swimming and diving and double-time marching with full packs—was grueling, exhausting, and extraordinarily effective. The message was loud and clear: to be an officer you had to lead by more than just the sound of your voice and the seat of your pants. And if you weren't in good physical shape when you arrived at the Academy, you sure as hell would be by the time regular classes started in the fall.

By the time lights out finally permitted the plebes to lay their heads back on their pillows, they were bone tired and one day closer to being real Navy men.

Even though the venerable old Academy was changing, opening itself up to groups previously excluded from the elite corps of midshipmen, the life of

a plebe at Annapolis was immutable. Like every one
of his classmates, David Robinson was yelled at, bullied, and abused. It was no surprise that by the end of
the summer they'd all just about had enough.

But their life at the Academy was just beginning.
Even after Plebe Summer was over, after the upperclassmen returned from their summer assignments
and vacations for another school year, life for a Naval
Academy plebe didn't get much easier.

In the fall, reveille was six-thirty instead of five
o'clock. In the next half hour, every midshipman was
expected to shave, shower, clean up his room, and
dress in time to fall in with his squad for morning
formation—the first of three each day—at seven
o'clock. The brigade of midshipmen was divided into
two regiments, six battalions, and thirty-six companies. Each company was divided into three platoons,
and each platoon into three squads. David's squad,
like all the others, was approximately 120 strong, and
consisted of a mixture of classes. And each senior (or
midshipman 1st class) who had the honor to serve as
squad leader made it clear to all the future officers
under his command that every member of the squad
was responsible to all the others, and that any screw-
up in discipline reflected on the entire unit.

Like any normal teenager, David had trouble adjusting to the strict limits placed on plebes, who were
forbidden to have radios, watch TV, date civilians, or
leave the yard except between noon and midnight on
Saturday. The lack of time to goof off, to go drinking
during the week, or to do any of the usual things that
disrupt a college freshman's studies made him won-

der at times whether he'd made the right choice of college.

But David put aside his misgivings; from the very beginning he was as gung ho as any plebe in the yard. He thrived under the discipline of the Academy: it was a place where academic achievement counted, where he could focus himself without the distraction of too much free time, and where he would eventually become what he wanted to be—an officer and a gentleman. He didn't even mind the three formations a day, or the occasional eight-hour shifts on a watch squad. He enjoyed the challenge of his academic courses—physics, math, computer science, and the rest—but like every midshipman, bridled at the homework, which he laughingly described as varying "from too much to way too much."

Military duties, said one coach who knew him well, "weren't as tough for David as for some other people. Because coming from a military background he knew what to expect, and because of his personality and his size he didn't really have anyone take advantage or harass him."

Along with the heavy academic load and military training came the mandatory phys ed courses: David's natural athletic abilities helped him ace gymnastics (he was even chosen to demonstrate some moves in front of his class); he also swam reasonably well (despite a not inconsequential fear of leaping off the 10-meter diving board); and he boxed, his long reach and quick feet making him a formidable opponent in the ring.

In addition to his daily three hours of military training, his grueling course work (which lasted from

seven-forty-five to noon, and resumed after noon formation and lunch for two more periods), his phys ed
instruction and his homework, David was also a
member of the varsity basketball team.

CHAPTER II

A RAW BEGINNER

By the time his elder son David was a senior in high school, Ambrose Robinson had retired from the Navy and was working as an independent contractor for the government in Washington, D.C. After a while, the commuting from Virginia Beach had become too much for him, so he moved his family up to Dale City, a middle-class community in Woodbridge, Virginia. David, though, remained in Virginia Beach to complete his degree at Green Run High School.

"But," he later said, "I found I missed my family, so I moved up."

At the time, David had no thoughts about playing varsity basketball. He had tried out for the Green Run team as a 5-9 freshman, but as he himself later admitted, "I wasn't very good." By the time he was a junior, David had sprouted all the way to 6-4, but he still had a lot more important things to think about than basketball: like computers, music, having fun, and making friends.

When David arrived in northern Virginia, he tried to register at nearby Garfield High. But he

found that instead he would have to travel each day
to Osbourn Park High School in Manassas. Even
though the school was over thirteen miles from his
home and the morning bus ride far from enjoyable,
Osbourn Park was much more manageable than
Green Run had been. It was smaller, much less competitive, and there were a lot fewer athletic kids his
size in this middle-class Washington suburb than
there had been down in the Tidewater area.

Osbourn Park was a clean, modern, low-slung
brick building with a sprawling campus. The football
stadium had lights for night play, and the parking lot
had enough space for hundreds of students to park
their cars. There was plenty of room for kids to practice their skateboard tricks—even though hotdogging
was strictly forbidden by school authorities.

David had begun the process of applying for the
Naval Academy well before he moved up from Virginia Beach, but soon after he enrolled in his new
school, his reasons for going to Annapolis became
more compelling. Because in a small suburban high
school like Osbourn Park, it was hard for basketball
coach Art Payne not to notice a 6'7" transfer student.

As soon as he saw David, Payne realized that "he
had a nice basketball body, the hands, the whole
thing," and he got "a little bit excited." Although it
was November 15th and the coach had already completed his final cuts, he asked the newcomer if he
would like to try out for the team. David said he
would, but explained that he didn't have shoes or
equipment with him. Even so, Payne asked David to
come to practice that afternoon, if only just to watch.
After classes that day, David came to the gym and

"he took his shoes off," recalled the coach with a smile. "You could tell he was anxious to play. I watched him catch the basketball a couple of times. Somebody said, 'Let's see you dunk the ball.' He took it and dunked—barefooted!"

The excited coach gave David a medical form and told him he needed a physical before he could join the team. "Sure enough," said Payne, "the next day he's standing there all ready to play."

It wasn't so much that David loved basketball. Actually, he preferred playing baseball, where, as a first baseman, his height helped him keep a lot of wild throws from turning into errors. He also liked football, loved to bowl, won a peewee golf tournament when he was twelve, and was an excellent gymnast. But despite his all-around athletic talent, David never wanted to be just a jock. He was an avid reader of science fiction, was passionate about playing the piano, and could disappear for hours programming a computer. Once, when he was fifteen and his father was away at sea, he built a six-foot projection screen television from a kit. But more than anything else, ever since he was little, David loved math. "When he was a kid," his father said, "his mother used to take him to the store and use him to figure out the price of things she bought by the ounce. He could add it up faster than a calculator."

With all of David's gifts and interests, basketball was not a priority. But he knew that playing a varsity sport was a great way to break the ice and make new friends fast.

"He just liked being around people," said Payne. "From the very start he wanted to be a part of the

team." As David's luck would have it, the day after
he put on a uniform Osbourn Park's starting center
injured himself and David took over his position.
Payne remembers that David "never missed a game,
never fouled out, and was a decent high school basketball player. If he'd been here the whole time, if
he'd played four years, he would've been a real good
high school basketball player."

Although he was far from being a superstar, he
could jump, he ran the floor well, and he had a pretty
good left-handed bank shot. Former Navy coach Paul
Evans remembers that because David lived right outside of Washington, one day "we got a call from a
retired Navy captain saying there's a kid over here
that's got 1300 on the boards, and he can run up and
down pretty good," and since "there was obviously a
push on at the Academy to bring in minority students" David became a natural recruiting prospect
for Navy.

The Academy's coaching staff frequently came
around to watch David play. They projected the 6-7
Osbourn Park center as an athletic small forward
along the lines of Richmond's Johnny Newman, who
was then the top player in Navy's league, the ECAC
South (later the Colonial Athletic Association). But
they weren't the only ones to come to Osbourn Park.
VMI (Virginia Military Institute) also made a good
case for themselves, and David took their interest
very seriously. The George Mason coaches came
around too. With an eye to his SAT scores, the Ivy
League schools suddenly tried to sell him on their
centuries-old traditions of excellence.

But for David the choice finally came down to

Navy or VMI. His father, thinking about the future, counseled David that he might not want to commit himself to five years of military service after graduation. But David looked at the commitment on the positive side: the Academy was guaranteeing him a good job after college—as a Naval officer. Another deciding factor, according to Coach Payne, was that "the Academy was an easy drive from Woodbridge, so he'd be able to see his folks much more often than if he went farther away to school."

When David arrived at Annapolis, the coaches considered him something of a project: he was obviously an excellent athlete, but with his lack of experience, he was hardly a Division 1 college basketball player. But then Navy wasn't a national power like Georgetown or Duke, either. In fact, until Paul Evans arrived, the Middies had spent two full decades without a winning record.

While the Navy football stadium was often full (and mandatory attendance at games was far from the only reason partisans whooped it up on the Annapolis gridiron), the ancient—and generally empty —5,000-seat Halsey Fieldhouse was the home of Navy hoops. And while the Middies always had their fair share of competitive teams and even an occasional All-American (including the great running back Joe Bellino and the legendary quarterback Roger Staubach) between the hashmarks, on the hardwood the Middies only occasionally rose to a level of mediocrity. Hoops was not the Midshipmen's game.

And with the Academy's height restrictions, no one ever expected it to be. Navy, everybody assumed,

would never be able to challenge the big-time basketball schools, either on the court or in the recruiting
arena. As a result, the Navy coaches could afford to
be patient with a raw but talented plebe.

Before Midshipman Robinson reported for his
first practice, Coach Evans and his assistants, Pete
Herrmann and Dave Laton, had high hopes that the
freshman's athletic ability and intelligence would allow him to make a tangible contribution to their improving program. And when he did show up, the
coaches noticed something else—David was still
growing. "He was pushing 6-9," says Evans, which
brought him an inch over the limit for a midshipman,
even with a waiver. But once you've been accepted by
the Academy, they can't throw you out for growing.
Suddenly Navy's small forward prospect was beginning to look a lot like a center.

The starting postman, Cliff Maurer, was even
taller than David (at 6-10-1/2, he had grown during
his Navy years to become the tallest midshipman in
history). He had also made himself into a pretty good
ballplayer, having worked his way from the j.v. to the
starting spot in the last two seasons. Cliff gave David
someone his size to practice against.

From the start, Evans brought David along
slowly, not wanting to scare off the raw, multifaceted
pivotman. But just before the start of the season,
David landed a left uppercut in boxing class—and
broke his wrist. He missed the first four games. And
when he rejoined the team, it took him a while to
adjust.

Although Navy wasn't playing anything like an
ACC or Big East schedule, at times David seemed a

little out of his league. "When he came in it was like teaching an eighth grader," Evans recalls. But while that meant he lacked a number of fundamental skills, it also meant "he didn't have a lot of bad habits, he didn't put the ball on the floor every time, he didn't do a lot of things that kids pick up in the playground. And he was eager to learn the game." Of course David, with only one year of organized basketball behind him, had a lot to learn.

One thing Evans demanded from his big men was aggressiveness. To help them develop fearlessness and the ability to mix it up under the boards, he had a rebounding drill in which he threw the ball off the rim, and, according to David, "all the big guys were supposed to go get the rebound." Matched up against Maurer and the Middies' best player, 6-7 Vernon Butler, "I got beat up every day. They're big boys," David said. "I caught a lot of elbows."

The skinny plebe got banged around and spent a lot of time protecting his nose. "It wasn't fun," he said, but it toughened him up. He soon learned to give as well as he got.

Evans played David sparingly, and whenever Maurer and David were in the lineup at the same time, the plebe was always positioned at the low post. "We didn't want David playing at more than one position," says Evans, "because we wanted to get him to do one thing well." Occasionally in practice he showed glimpses of more than promise—at those times, David's quickness made him virtually unstoppable. But as often as not, he would play as though his mind was somewhere else; he lacked both intensity and concentration on the court. Still, Evans was patient.

Everywhere David went, he soaked up new experiences and learned from them. Assistant Coach Dave Laton remembered that when the Middies went to Hawaii to play in the early season Rainbow Classic, the tall plebe's teammates called him "Country" because he'd never been on a plane or in a hotel room before. The coaching staff also worked steadily with him on developing his skills. "We always used him on the left side because he started out with a great left-handed bank shot," says Evans, but in practice, the coaches kept him working on his hook, on going to the middle, and on his defense. Because the low-key Navy program competed in a low-profile league, it was also easy for David to build his confidence in game situations. "He didn't have a seven-footer to go against every night," recalls Evans, and his height advantage enabled him to feel good about his progress.

According to Evans, David's decision to stay close to home also made a big difference. "One thing that really helped him at the Academy was that his mom, his dad and Chuckie [David's younger brother] were able to get down for all the games; they were able to get down there on Saturdays, and he was able to keep that closeness with his family which he always had. Almost every Saturday morning his dad was there watching him at practice."

Probably the most important game of David's freshman season was one his family didn't get to see. He was still no more than lukewarm about basketball when the Midshipmen traveled up to Connecticut to play Fairfield. He played less than a half, but scored twelve points and was ecstatic. Assistant Coach Pete Herrmann asked him why, and he replied, "Coach, I can't remember getting more than nineteen in high school!" But it wasn't just Midshipman Robinson who was happy about his performance. Paul Evans recalls that "it was at about that point that we pretty much realized he had *some* talent."

By the end of the season, a lot of people were impressed by David's progress. His high school coach Art Payne "couldn't believe how much he improved," and with an average of 7.6 points and 4 rebounds in less than 13 minutes a game, David was selected as the ECAC's South Rookie of the Year.

Paul Evans had coached Navy to a 24-8 record, the first twenty-win season in the school's history. Looking ahead to the next year, he saw an even better team, with Midshipman Robinson joining established players like power forward Vernon Butler and long-range bomber Kylor Whitaker as a starter.

But despite the coaching staff's plans, the eighteen-year-old plebe was still plagued by doubts about whether he even wanted to continue playing basketball. He had so many other interests, and he really didn't think he was as good as the coaches thought he was.

Paul Evans sat down with David and "tried to explain to him what the possibilities were." Already the coach could see a star in the making—possibly even a future pro. David was now 6-10—a true big man—and he was still growing, but at the same time he had the all-around athletic ability of a small forward. "David," Evans said, "I don't think I've ever

seen anybody with as much potential as you and I
think maybe you should play the cards out and give it
a little bit more effort.''

Finally David agreed. He didn't want basketball
to interfere with the rest of his life, but he owed it to
himself to see how good a player he could become.

CHAPTER III

SUDDENLY
SEVEN FEET TALL

Midshipman Robinson's plebe year was finally over.
He was free at last of the yard, and looked forward to
spending three whole months away from Annapolis.

His first year at the Academy had been pretty
much of a success. He'd maintained a B average,
which wasn't easy in a major like math. He'd picked
up the military stuff pretty well, and at times he actually enjoyed the marching, the formations, and the
discipline. He had made a lot of friends. And he'd
gotten much better in basketball. But more than anything else, he'd just made it through. He'd never be a
plebe again.

David had also learned quite a bit about himself,
and about how hard he'd have to work to be the best
at anything—Navy was not high school. Sometimes
he'd felt bone tired, and the extra effort didn't seem
to be worth it. There were times, particularly on the
basketball court, when he just felt like giving up. The
coaches always seemed to ride him more than anyone

else. But he knew, deep down, that their prodding
had something to do with how much he'd grown as a
player. Still, David liked to hang out and shoot the
breeze with some of the other guys a lot more than he
liked working on the basketball court. He'd watch his
friend, Hoosier Carl Liebert from Floyds Knob, Indiana, go back onto the basketball court in his few minutes of free time to work on his moves and his shooting. Sometimes he couldn't believe how Carl was
always ready to go out and work. He preferred to
hang out and socialize.

David had always expected to be the best at everything, and in fact he was quite good at almost
everything he tried. There were times, though, when
his success was less than immediate and he got frustrated. In his freshman year in high school he had
quit basketball rather than ride the bench. Even
though he felt the urge to do the same thing now, the
coaches kept telling him he had the potential to be a
great player, and what they were saying finally began
to sink in. With his size, speed, and jumping ability,
maybe it was worth concentrating on this game after
all.

Most promising college basketball players spend
their summers playing ball—period. Some take a few
summer school courses. Others get temporary jobs to
help them supplement their scholarships and make
ends meet. But things are a little different for a basketball player at the Naval Academy. Summer is not
exactly free time. For a good part of his three-month
"vacation," David was on duty in the Navy.

David spent the summer after his freshman year,
"youngster summer" in Naval Academy parlance, in

a variety of activities. There was a one-month mandatory cruise, and another month when military training was required, but the specifics of the assignment were optional. He thought he'd like to try submarine duty, but once he did, he found that fitting his long frame into a sub was quite a job. Somebody even made a crack about cutting a hole in the top of the sub and using him as a periscope. For his one free month, David decided to follow Coach Evans' advice and concentrate on basketball. He started pumping iron to add a little bulk to his 195-pound frame. And he joined Washington's Urban Coalition League, where he held his own—averaging 17 points in five games—against pretty tough competition.

When midshipman third class, 14th company, third battalion, first regiment David Maurice Robinson returned to the yard in the fall, he was 20 pounds heavier, a lot stronger, and a far more confident basketball player.

At first nothing much appeared to have changed. He still had a demanding course load, still rose with the entire brigade at 0630 hours and fell in for morning colors when the Enterprise Bell (taken from the bridge of the famed World War II aircraft carrier) rang, and still felt totally at home in cavernous Bancroft Hall, with its five miles of labyrinthine corridors and 65,000-square-foot dining hall. But once basketball practice started, it was clear things were different.

David hadn't started a single game as a plebe, and the Middies had still won twenty-four games. Now Coach Evans, the architect of the program's turnaround over the last two years, was telling the team that he wanted them to be even better—and the coach wanted David to be one of the cornerstones on Navy's first tournament team in three decades. That was a lot of pressure to put on a nineteen-year-old kid who'd only been playing competitive basketball for two years. Still, David himself could see, from the first practice, how much he'd improved, and how dominant he could be when he asserted himself.

Navy, like the other service academies and the Ivy League schools, had always been a ball-control team. But Evans, responding in part to his personnel, in part to his own instincts, junked that part of Navy tradition and put in a new system. With both David, now 6-11, and the 6-7, 235-pound Vernon Butler pounding the boards, Evans thought the Middies could rebound with anyone. In preseason practice he put more stress on the transition game and instituted a controlled fast-break style offense, with David setting up at the low post whenever Navy had to go into its half-court game.

Soon after the season began, it was clear that David had arrived—as a *force.* He was the difference in a double overtime 74-71 victory at Lafayette despite a lackluster first half in which he took just three shots and frustrated the coaching staff with his lack of concentration and aggressiveness. After the intermission, David completely dominated the action. He sank five second-half buckets, added three in the first overtime and put in the go-ahead basket in the second extra session. His performance seemed to prove that Coach Evans was right: he could be the Middies' go-to guy in the clutch. But Lafayette coach Butch Van Breda Kolff wasn't so sure. "We had guys 6-6 and 6-7 guarding him," he remarked, skeptical about David's ability to "make that little shot against big guys."

A poor game at Penn State proved nothing. It was disappointing to everybody on the team, but Evans felt maybe David "was embarrassed a little bit." If he was, the experience motivated him to focus on the game more, to play more aggressively and confidently.

David's big turnaround came immediately, in a four-team holiday tournament at Southern Illinois University called the Saluki Shootout. Playing against the host team's 6-11 Kenny Perry in the tournament opener, David scored 31 points and grabbed 13 rebounds. (Navy still lost by three.) The next night he put up even more impressive numbers—37 points and 18 rebounds—in a victory over Western Illinois.

People noticed. His performance was lauded in every major area newspaper. *Sports Illustrated* named him its "Player of the Week." Some observers even went so far as to mention him in the same breath as the Washington area's resident superstar, Georgetown's Patrick Ewing.

Coach Evans, predicting even better things to come, declared, "I'm not really surprised."

"Toward the end of last year," he said, David "was getting 15–20 points in 18–19 minutes. He's still struggling some on defense but he is an amazing athlete for his size. And he's just in his third year of learning the game. The more he learns, the more he'll be able to do."

David himself struggled to put his newfound fame into perspective. "My life still doesn't center on

basketball," he told *The Richmond News Leader,*
"but it is moving more and more in that direction."
Later, he described the experience as "pretty incredi-
ble. It was the first time I got an idea of what I could
do."

After the Saluki Shootout, the Middies, with a
4-2 record, started a four-week break for exams. The
breather not only gave David some time to study, but
also a chance to think about what was happening to
him.

□

In less than two and a half years, the midshipman had
gone from being an unknown—a beginner at basketball—to the national spotlight. People were seriously
talking about the possibility of his becoming a pro
ballplayer. It was, as David liked to say, a real trip.

It was hard to keep it all in perspective, to remain in touch with why he had chosen to go to Annapolis in the first place. But David was a midshipman; he had come to Navy for its academic program
and for its career opportunities. He promised himself
he wouldn't let those things slide. He buckled down
and studied, finishing the first semester with a 3.22
average. And he proceeded full steam ahead for the
spring term, registering for eighteen credit hours in
thermodynamics, navigation, advanced calculus,
physics, and computer science.

Evans later recalled that back in practice that
winter, "You saw glimpses, you saw times where he'd
just come down and score seven, eight times straight
and no one could stop him. He had a great turnaround bank shot where he could just get the ball at

the block, turn and shoot it up off the board with his left hand and nobody could really get near him."

Those dominating stretches in practice helped David to increase his confidence, and when the Middies returned to action, they were virtually unbeatable. Naturally, the focus of attention was on the skinny seven footer who'd come literally out of nowhere to become a star. But the Navy squad was far from a one-man show. The Middies had solid, intelligent, fundamentally sound players at every position. And in large measure, the coach was able to devise strategies that both maximized their strengths and hid their weaknesses.

Evans believed that "Vernon [Butler] was the key guy in terms of turning the program around." Butler, a junior, was a perfect complement to the electrifying, quick as a cat sophomore center. He was a bruising, blue-collar-type power forward who averaged 11.6 points and 10.2 rebounds in his freshman year, and who led the Middies as a sophomore with 14.7 points and 8.7 rebounds per game. His effectiveness under the boards could not be underestimated: by the end of the season he would be third in the nation among juniors in career rebounds, behind only Wayman Tisdale and Karl Malone.

Kylor Whitaker attributed the Middies' success to "Coach Evans and the chemistry of the team." He was aware that Navy was "not like [#1-ranked] Georgetown. They're a team of great individual athletes with outstanding basketball skills. They run, jump and know how to play physically." On the other hand, he continued, "We need all the parts to be successful. We complement each other. Vernon

and David are our inside players. I'm an outside
shooter with some rebounding skills. Doug [Wojcik]
doesn't shoot a lot, he's our passer, who tries to get
the ball inside and Cliff [Rees] plays the tough defense. He is matched against the top backcourt scorers."

Another big factor in the Middies' success was
Evans' 2-3 zone defense, which compensated for
Navy's athletic deficiencies and enabled them to be-
come one of the nation's leaders in shooting defense.

All coaches know that the commonality of focus
of a successful team is very fragile. A bruised ego,
lack of recognition, or a swelled head could easily
upset the balance and turn a winner into just another
group of selfish players. Coach Evans knew that
Navy's success was a team effort—but he was also
aware that the press would hone in on the phenom in
the low post. He was determined not to allow that
attention to detract from the smooth functioning of
the squad.

Evans needn't have been concerned. As he later
recalled, "David is so intelligent you could say things
to him like, 'You're gonna get all the publicity, you're
the star, you better do what you can to make the rest
of the guys feel equal to you, you better keep your
head in place.' One of the things he did very well was
stay within the framework of the team and keep
things at an even keel where all that sudden publicity
could have really gone to his head and made him
someone a lot of the kids didn't want to be around.
The ego thing didn't affect him."

David strived to maintain his own balance, de-

spite the winning streak, the sudden publicity, and
the talk about his pro potential.

"I never thought of myself as a big-time basketball player," he told *The Sporting News* early in January. "I still don't really. In high school, basketball
was just something I sort of experimented with. It
was never that big a thing to me. Now, I work hard at
it because I think I have the potential to be good. But
if I don't become a big star, it isn't that big a deal to
me. I still play for fun."

While the tall teenager was trying to enjoy himself, the word of mouth about David Robinson and
the Midshipmen was spreading rapidly to every corner of the country. Everybody, it seemed, wanted to
see them, to know if this cleancut kid and his crewcut
teammates were for real. CBS responded by putting
them on national TV.

Questions began to be raised about David's future. If he left the Academy after the sophomore year,
he would have no military commitment; he could
choose any career road he wanted. But if he returned
to Annapolis as a junior, he would be committing
himself to five years of Navy service after graduation.

An interview with Navy's tallest midshipman was
the focus of the halftime show during Navy's January
1985 game on CBS. When asked about his plans,
David replied, "I'm very happy here. I honestly never
thought about the possibilities of playing in the pros
when I came but when people start talking about it,
you can't help but have it on your mind. Playing basketball for money," he continued, "for two or three
hundred thousand dollars a year, that sounds like the
best life of all."

He thought about the money and the fame, but
whenever he started to get too carried away with his
new fantasy, the Naval Academy was there to remind
him of his responsibilities. When the Middies finally
saw their winning streak broken—at eleven games
(by George Mason)—David still had a pretty good
game, with 25 points, 12 rebounds, and 7 blocks. But
he had no time to dwell on either his stats or the
team's defeat: he went back to his room in Bancroft
Hall that Thursday night knowing that on Friday he
had three tests. Each day at Morning Colors, no matter what happened the night before, David was expected to stand ramrod straight, in full dress uniform. He was still just one of five thousand
midshipmen eating his meals in Mother B's mess hall.
And he wasn't exempted from other duties, either;
like every middie, David had to salute his superiors,
attend mandatory training sessions, and stand his
turn at watch.

At home in the yard, nothing had changed. Nothing that is, except that the place was going crazy. "I
have been a Navy basketball watcher since the mid-
1930s," remarked town alderman and *Annapolis
Capital* sports editor Al Hopkins. "There has never
been so much interest and excitement in a Navy
team."

The perennially empty seats at Halsey Fieldhouse
had disappeared. Spectators stopped going outside to
look at the harbor, and began to pay attention to the
action on the court. On Saturday nights when the
team was playing at home, middies, instead of abandoning ship, stayed in the yard and gave up some of

their precious free time to watch David & Co. play. Attendance at Navy games more than doubled.

The Robinsons themselves were among the most rabid and regular Navy rooters. Driving into Annapolis in a car with Virginia license plates that read NA-50-VY, they were an unmistakable private family-cheering-section for David at almost every home game. Ambrose, a big, 6'5" bear of a man, would arrive at the Academy wearing his Navy sweatshirt, inevitably with his wife Freda, who would constantly shout encouragement to her boy on the court. Along for the ride would be the backflipping fifteen-year-old Middie ballboy Chuckie, David's younger brother. And as often as possible. David's older sister Kimberly, a 21-year-old Howard senior, would join the rest of the clan in the Navy stands.

□

The day before the contest every midshipman considers the biggest of the year—Navy's war against Army —Tecumseh was wearing his warpaint, prepared for battle. When each middie passed by the gussied-up symbol of the Academy on his way across the yard, he invariably stopped to give the Indian warrior a left-handed salute, and reached into his pocket to pull out some pennies to shower upon the chief as a victory offering. Navy was 20-4, sitting atop the ECAC's Southern Division and highly favored, but a middie can't take anything for granted—especially against Army.

The night of the big game the Navy officials were faced with over 6,000 midshipmen, cadets and interested observers all hoping to get into Halsey. The

capacity of the old fieldhouse was listed as 4,700, but
the Academy wanted to accommodate everyone they
could, and by game time every nook and cranny was
filled and the noise was deafening. It reached a cre-
scendo when No. 50's name was announced.

From the opening tap, the competition was
fierce. Army, led by their star sophomore guard
Kevin Houston, slowed the pace to a crawl, thus ne-
gating Midshipman Robinson's quickness. But David
still dominated. He was a one-man naval aircraft carrier, and even though the smaller Cadets sagged inside in an attempt to deny him the ball down on the
block, their efforts were in vain. In many ways,
Army's game plan was successful. The skirmish
would have gone exactly as they had planned—except
for David. He scored 32 points and controlled the
boards with 14 rebounds. Army put up a good fight,
but in the end Navy prevailed, 48-47. It was a typical,
hard-fought Army-Navy game.

As the season went on, the Middies continued to
win, and David continued to star. And although the
questions about his future were becoming more and
more urgent, he and his teammates tried not to let
themselves be distracted from the business at hand.

Navy hadn't gone to the NCAA tournament since
1960. Despite their impressive record, the Middies
knew that in order to be assured of a berth in 1985,
they had to win their conference championship. (The
year before, Richmond had won the ECAC South title and the automatic spot. Navy, meanwhile, had
been sorely disappointed, not even getting an NIT bid
despite their 24-8 record.) Even though Richmond
had beaten Auburn, with Charles Barkley and Chuck

Person, in last year's tourney, and even though David
had brought this year's Midshipmen a good deal of
national recognition, the Navy coaches had to assume
that only one team from their conference would be
selected for this year's field. While Evans "poli-
ticked" to cover his bases and ensure an NIT bid, the
players concentrated on winning their way into the
NCAA.

At the end of the regular season, Navy was tied
with defending conference champ Richmond for the
league lead with an 11-3 record. But with an overall
record of 26-6, the Middies drew the first seed in the
conference tournament, which was to be played on
three consecutive days starting on March 7th at William and Mary College.

On the first night, Navy breezed over the league's
worst team, East Carolina, with David shooting a
perfect 12 for 12 from the field. Next they met the
home team, and were surprised by the tough fight
William and Mary put up before finally going down
to an 89-83 defeat. Finally, the Middies met the Richmond Spiders, who had blown them out in the 1984
conference championship game while holding Plebe
Robinson to a mere 5 points before he fouled out.
This time Richmond again spun its web around the
Midshipmen, taking a 44-39 halftime lead on the hot
shooting of Kelvin Johnson and Johnny Newman. But
in the second half Navy adjusted. They banged away
inside, getting the ball to Butler time and again when
his man double teamed the Middies' main man. By
the final buzzer, Vernon and David had combined for
53 points, as Navy won a hard-earned nine-point victory.

The Middies were in the NCAAs!

On March 15th in Dayton, Ohio, the United States Naval Academy made its first appearance in college basketball's national championship tournament in a quarter of a century. They were seeded thirteenth in their region, and given little chance to defeat the Southeastern Conference's regular season champ L.S.U. But once again Navy unleashed its big guns. David was a terror off the boards, and the Middie zone forced the Tigers, a weak perimeter-shooting team, into an outside game and 34 percent shooting. The total demolition of Dale Brown's heavily favored squad caused the L.S.U. coach to reflect, "These are the moments when you wonder why you coach."

Two nights later the Middies were back on the court, this time against their neighbors from the University of Maryland. Again Navy was a heavy underdog, and once more they came out strong. By early in the second half, David had 20 points and the Midshipmen had a 45-34 lead. Maryland Coach Lefty Dreisell called a timeout; he switched his team's defensive assignments, ordering his own powerful big man, All-American forward Len Bias, onto the young Navy center with instructions to put some muscle on the Middie star. With a full-court press helping to deny David the ball down in the lane, and Bias using his strength to push him out of position in the low post, David became a nonfactor. The Terrapins came back, and the weary Middies couldn't hold on. With 4:45 to play, Bias raced in off the weak side and put home a monster jam of a missed shot to give Maryland their first lead of the game, 58-57. After a TV timeout, the Terps went into a four-corner stall, and the Middies didn't challenge them again until there was less than a minute left. When Maryland's Jeff Adkins made both ends of a one-and-one with forty seconds remaining, the game—and Navy's season—was all but over.

"Emotionally, I think we were out of gas," David said later. "When they made their run, we were hanging on. You don't win by hanging on."

Still, David and the rest of the Midshipmen returned to the yard as conquering heroes: they had put together the finest basketball season in Naval Academy history.

As he graciously received the pats on the back, high fives, and congratulations from all his buddies in Bancroft Hall, the irresistible force behind the Middies' success was still wrestling with the problem that had been plaguing him since Christmas. He was a math major, and preferred logical, precise answers. But there didn't seem to be any easily definable solution this time. In just two short years at the Academy, the equation of his life had shifted radically: now just about everyone was telling him he had pro potential, and the five-year Navy service commitment suddenly loomed, not as a career opportunity, but as an impediment to his future. Whatever he decided to do, he knew he'd have to give something up. He also knew that the time was fast approaching when he had to make the choice about whether to return to Annapolis for another go-round.

CHAPTER IV

DOING THE
RIGHT THING

Life had been so much simpler for David when he
was younger. Unlike many of his peers, who grew up
questioning their families, their values, even their
place in the world, David's childhood allowed for no
such ambiguity. In the Robinson home, everything
always seemed to make sense. Decisions were clear-
cut, and on those rare occasions when he had trouble
figuring something out for himself, his parents were
invariably there to help.

Now, though, as David approached his twentieth
birthday, everything was suddenly more complex.
Since very early in his sophomore season, he had
been wrestling with the question: should he stay at
the Academy or should he leave? For once, he was
faced with a decision that was not black and white,
right or wrong. It was filled with gray areas. It was a
struggle.

David was well aware that many midshipmen—
perhaps a third of his class—would withdraw from

the Academy for one reason or another at the end of the school year. They would leave Annapolis scot free, with no commitment to serve. Some would go because they simply didn't want to be in the Navy for five years, others because they had an aversion to the Academy's 24-hour-a-day military discipline, while more than a few just couldn't cut the academic mustard. He certainly had more incentive than most to quit. If he wanted to, he could transfer to virtually any school in the country and be welcomed with open arms, and a full scholarship. He could also pursue basketball as a career.

But David liked Navy. He liked the atmosphere in the hall, the feeling of working toward a defined goal and building something. He liked his friends and the academic atmosphere. In short, he was comfortable at the Academy. "This is a good school, and it will take a lot to get me out of here," he said. "The money offered in the pros is very attractive, so I can't really say I'm not going to give it a chance. It would be fun to play as a career. But I can't let that get into my eyes and cloud what a degree from here would mean."

Navy life was a sure thing. It was a good job, a proud tradition, a secure career path. Basketball, on the other hand, was fraught with uncertainties.

"I can't see myself as a Ewing," David explained to *Sports Illustrated,* "and if I spent all my time playing basketball, I might not enjoy it. My father says basketball's a transient thing," he continued. "When you graduate [from Navy], you get a good job and a pension after twenty years. I like the saying in our home-game program: 'Some college students learn what to do from nine to five. Midshipmen learn what to do from twenty-two to forty-seven.' " For the nine-teen-year-old midshipman third class, becoming a Navy man like his father seemed to be a perfectly natural decision.

Still, with so much at stake, he had to think about his other options. Everyone in the media was filling him with stories about what a great future he had as a basketball player, building him up as a certain NBA draft choice. And while he wasn't totally convinced, he was affected by what people said.

"It bothers me," he told one observer in January. "I sit around and it distracts me from other things at the Academy . . . when I'm on watch I daydream about it. It's kind of bad that the whole thing was brought up now." Often, when he began to feel at loose ends, he wished basketball would just go away.

According to Navy Coach Evans, there was a great deal of pressure on David to transfer. His young star got some letters and phone calls, the coach said, "that shouldn't have been made" concerning his plans for the future. Numerous schools—from the ACC, the Big Ten and other major basketball confer-ences—while not directly "recruiting" David, also made their interest known. Schools like UCLA, Georgetown, Kentucky, and Duke were all men-tioned as possible destinations for the Navy center. Virginia was mentioned as a contender in the Robin-son lottery, too, although Cavalier Coach Terry Hol-land called Navy to tell Evans that he would not pur-sue the Middies' center unless David decided to transfer. And when Robinson's name was mentioned at a Madison Square Garden doubleheader, Notre

Dame coach Digger Phelps said, "If he leaves Navy, we'll take him." It seemed as if just about everybody was interested in Midshipman Robinson. Two years into his college career, he was the hottest recruiting prize in the country.

David realized that remaining at Navy could torpedo any possibility of a career in professional basketball. The Academy's service commitment would mean five years away from the game, and even if he continued to get better through his senior year, it would be extremely difficult to come back at the age of twenty-seven.

There was some uncertainty, however, as to whether he'd end up actually having to serve. David may have believed that, because of his height, he would be released from his commitment. There was speculation that an accommodation could be reached that would allow him to do both—go to Navy and play pro ball. But there were no guarantees.

The bottom line was that he understood perfectly the implications of a decision to stay at the Academy, although at times he didn't seem to care. Particularly since it seemed to be the decision Ambrose Robinson really wanted his son to make.

□

David Robinson worshiped his father, and looked to him as the ultimate authority figure. Years later he said, "I never had sports role models. The only person I ever saw anything in was my dad. I'd look at him and say, 'Wow, how'd you get to be a father? You go to Dad School or something?'"

David's feelings were reciprocated by his parents' loving and protective attitude toward their son. Whatever else happened in his life, he could be sure that his mom and dad had his best interests at heart. For as long as he could remember, it had always been that way.

For his parents, David had been special ever since he was a baby. When he was six months old, his mother took him to visit a relative in New Hampshire. Suddenly she heard crying coming from the bedroom—crying that stopped suddenly, inexplicably. Freda rushed back into the room. "I didn't see David on the bed," she said. "I thought Mitchell (her brother-in-law) had the baby. He didn't.

"Then I looked and saw the tip of David's head squeezed between the bed and the wall. He was turning blue . . . I thought he was dead."

Frantic and praying for a miracle, she looked for a sign of life in her infant son's small body. "I couldn't feel a pulse," she said. "I started to give him CPR and I could hear his little lungs. Then he started to go into convulsions."

After David was taken to the hospital, the doctor told his parents that it could be a long time before they knew whether he suffered brain damage.

For years, his parents watched his development, measuring him against other kids. And by the time he was in first grade, it was clear: he was not only normal, he was gifted.

Now, as the season progressed and the pressure grew, David knew his father would be there for him.

Ambrose Robinson's involvement in his son's decision was hardly something that came out of the blue. Although his duties as a Chief Petty Officer meant he was often away at sea for weeks at a time, when he was home he made it a point to be involved in his children's lives. He would take his family on vacation and spend time fishing or bowling with his older son. When they were together, Ambrose would listen to his son's problems and offer his advice.

He had always been a good listener, the best person for his son to bounce ideas off of. But Ambrose had also always insisted that his son be responsible for his own choices.

"We're going to wait until after the season is over," he told the press, "and then if David asks me for help, I will help him. But it's his decision. I will support him one way or the other."

Ambrose and Freda Robinson spent most of their adult lives trying to ensure that their kids would not suffer from the same kind of overt prejudice they had experienced growing up. They wanted Kimberly, David, and Chuckie to have opportunities, and felt that Mr. Robinson's career in the Navy guaranteed rights for their children that they themselves never had.

As a girl growing up in South Carolina, Freda Robinson had been bused to a rundown and inferior blacks-only school; Ambrose was a high school junior in Little Rock when then-Arkansas-Governor Orval Faubus barred the door of the state capital's Central High to black students to prevent the desegregation of the city's schools. As a child Ambrose knew the effects of racism first-hand—his brother Kenneth had to endure the pressure of being the first black basketball player at Little Rock Central. Ambrose himself was frequently faced with situations where he was judged—solely on the basis of his skin color—to be less capable than he really was. Once, in high school, he was accused of cheating on a standardized achievement test because his scores eclipsed those of most of the white children in the school district, and he was ordered to take the test again to verify the results. Alone in a strictly monitored classroom, he did even better.

The racism he and his wife suffered as children led him to join the Navy, where there were at least some guarantees of equal treatment.

Like most middle-class parents, Ambrose and Freda felt there was nothing their kids couldn't do. They stressed the values of hard work and discipline, and told their kids that "anything in life is attainable if you want it badly enough."

With their father at sea and their mother working full-time as a nurse, everyone in the household had chores to do. And they couldn't just do the minimum to get by: doing the yard meant trimming the hedges, not just cutting the grass.

The children were expected to earn their own spending money—David worked a paper route and mowed lawns—and to do well in school. "Once in junior high," David recalled, "I got an A, two B's and a C and was grounded for six weeks for the C."

In an attempt to guarantee that their kids would receive the best possible education, the Robinsons lived in mostly white areas, and the children attended mostly white schools. They weren't told about their own parents' youthful struggles with racism. And they grew up thinking they were just like everyone else. "I was always in gifted classes with whites," said David. "It never dawned on me I was black."

Despite his parents' efforts to protect him, David wasn't totally insulated. Once, when he was sixteen, he went to a party thrown by the daughter of a white noncommissioned officer. When the kids started playing spin the bottle, as the only black kid at the party, he was asked to "referee." He was shocked to find out that he was not, after all, "one of them."

"I'd never really spent a lot of time around blacks, so socially, I was kind of backward. I really didn't know where I belonged."

In general, though, David felt at ease in his surroundings. And while he was occasionally awkward in social situations, he never lacked for confidence in the classroom, where he had a reputation among his peers as being a math and science whiz.

Because of David's obvious talents, Ambrose always assumed his older son would be a doctor or a physicist, and until he blossomed into a sudden star on the basketball court, he never gave a thought to the possibility that David might become a professional athlete. Even with David's newfound stature as a sports celebrity, he still didn't take pro basketball seriously as a career for his son. "You don't think of sports when you have a kid like David," he declared proudly.

Now, as his son approached a major turning point in his life, Ambrose did what he had always done. He listened, offered his advice, and protected David as much as possible. And while Ambrose always said the decision about remaining at the Academy was ultimately David's, he also made his own preferences quite clear.

"Personally," he told the press, "I hope there is no talk about transferring."

□

Paul Evans hoped the same thing. Under his tutelage David was rapidly becoming a great athlete and an integral part of a powerful team. Evans had some good reasons to be confident that his star player would remain at Navy: he knew the Robinson family and was aware of their priorities. He also knew that their son was not exactly basketball crazy. "David likes basketball," his coach said, "but he's not like Butler, who spends hours and hours in the gym during the off-season. If you push him too hard, he might stop enjoying it, and you don't want that. . . . he likes the game, but I don't think he wants to live it."

Evans was also aware that his star player's parents had met several times with Navy brass. He knew that the Naval Academy had promised to be "fair." David meant a lot to Navy—his presence guaranteed the Academy a lot more than just the income they were likely to receive from increased gate receipts and NCAA tournament shares; he was worth his weight in gold in good press. You couldn't imagine a better advertisement than this seven-foot-natural-wonder-math-major-electronics-whiz. And Evans knew that if the brass was inflexible, their walking billboard would be gone in a New York minute.

But none of the Navy's assurances lessened the pressures on David, nor did they make his decision automatic. The coach, who yelled at his star almost daily in practice and spent a lot of his own time trying to figure out how to motivate him, understood that David was under a great deal of stress. Evans told David that if the distractions became too much to handle that he would be there for him. But otherwise he was scrupulous about keeping his hands off.

Weeks went by as David pondered the variables. "I stayed out of it as far as the military part was concerned," Coach Evans recalled. Despite his own personal interests, "I told him it had to be his decision. He didn't owe me anything and he didn't owe the Academy anything; it had to be something he wanted to do one way or the other, because you didn't want him looking back a couple of years or ten years later and say I wish I'd done it the other way and I would have if I'd made my own decision. I don't think we wanted to put any pressure on him to stay and we really didn't."

After the NCAA loss to Maryland in March, Robinson returned to the yard along with the rest of the team. He was clearly optimistic about the next season's Navy squad, telling people that "We have everybody coming back next year." But at the same time he hedged on saying whether he was definitely returning, and was unable to do more than promise that he'd finish thinking it through soon.

David didn't want to make a hasty decision that he would later regret. He spoke to his friends—his roommate, Carl Leibert, and other teammates—and they listened and offered their opinions. He even talked with representatives of some of the schools courting him. And he went to his father for help.

Ambrose suggested that David write down the pluses and minuses on both sides of the question. And although David never did put it in writing, he thought seriously about what he stood to gain or lose from either course of action.

Before he made his mind up, he joined his father and his uncle, a Washington, D.C. Circuit Court judge, for a skull session. "My dad and my uncle just laid the whole thing out for me," David said. "Then they let me juggle with it."

David's uncle told him that if he transferred to a traditional basketball power, he would face top-flight competition game after game, and that he'd improve his skills much faster. And as a Washingtonian, he was of course a strong supporter of Georgetown and the Hoyas' charismatic coach, John Thompson. Georgetown, he pointed out, combined excellent academics and a basketball program that had gone to the national finals three times in four years. He reminded David that with Patrick Ewing moving on to the pros, the Hoyas would welcome him with open arms.

But if David was going to transfer, he didn't want to narrow his choices down too far. Along with Georgetown, he also seriously considered the merits of both Kentucky and UCLA.

There was also the question of money. If David continued improving, he could stand to make millions in the pros. But, he said, "I don't live for money. I mean, it's important to me. But a lot of people think you are automatically happy if you have a lot of money. I don't necessarily believe that is true. Money is a factor in what I do, but not a big motivating factor."

On the other side of the ledger, David had some pretty good things going for him in Annapolis. His studies were as important to him as ever, and even though some other schools offered a similarly challenging curriculum, he felt that nobody could give him a better education.

He also felt committed to the Academy and to his friends and teammates. He'd been brought up with a sense of loyalty and he couldn't just turn his back on a lifetime of values.

Besides, despite all the hoopla, he wasn't sure how good a basketball player he was going to be. If he didn't get any better—if he wasn't really good enough to make the pros—he'd still have his degree and his guaranteed job in the Navy. He didn't want to transfer, lose what he had, and find that he had made the move for nothing.

Other Navy men, he knew, had managed to combine their service with pro sports (most notably the great Heisman Trophy and all-pro quarterback Roger Staubach). But David was realistic; he knew it wasn't easy to come back from a five-year layoff.

Another factor tipping the scales in Navy's favor was the NCAA rule that required a transfer to lose a year of eligibility. David was just getting good at the game, still learning, and he was sure that sitting out a year would hold back his progress. Then he'd have only one year left to make an impression on the pros.

He was also scared. What if he made a wrong decision? What if he wasn't comfortable? What if the school he transferred to had another center who was better than he was?

Finally it came down to a matter of priorities.

And when he balanced everything out, his priorities had not changed.

On April 3rd, Midshipman Third Class David Robinson announced that he would finish his college education at the United States Naval Academy. In the end, he decided that he didn't want to put his whole life—present and future—into basketball.

The decision, he told *The Sporting News,* "was close. There are a lot of things about the Academy that I don't like. But I also know that anywhere you go there are going to be things you don't like. I thought a lot about what I would be giving up if I left —the education, the friendships, and the people. That would have been hard."

In an official statement released by the Naval Academy Athletic Association, David said, "After a great deal of thought and discussion with my parents, I've decided to remain here. The Academy has been good for me and I want the chance to receive a degree from here. I like the place and I like the people. From a basketball standpoint, I want to improve on what we accomplished this year. I'd like to be a part of the best basketball team the Naval Academy has ever had.

"If I had transferred, I would have had to sit out a year and that didn't sound real attractive. This way, I can play with my friends and I'll be in a program that I'm comfortable with. I'm happy with my decision and am already looking forward to next season. Pro ball? I guess I still have a hard time visualizing myself playing at that level, with all those great players."

Continuing, he said, "Everyone is saying I'm

great, but who can you listen to? I'm in control. I'm doing what I want to do. I have no regrets.

"I came here for academics. But all my goals got cloudy. The press confused me a bit.

"Basketball came so fast. It really just came together this year. I'm still in my early stages. If I had been better last year, I would have put more consideration into transferring. I don't know how much basketball means to me right now."

The decision pleased his parents, who told him how glad they were that he had decided to stay and become a Naval officer. It also pleased his teammates and friends at the Academy. His closest friend at school, Carl Leibert, said, "If you know David, you knew there was no doubt. He has a lot of pride about himself, and I mean not necessarily as a basketball player or a black person, but as an intelligent individual. A diploma from here means more to him than the millions he could have made. He is motivated by his own self-esteem."

And his decision transformed one of the most talked-about players in college basketball into a phenomenon.

□

That summer, David tried to squeeze his seven-foot-long body into a six-foot-long submarine berth, he sailed for a week on a small Navy craft, and he trudged through nail-tough Marine training at Quantico. Everywhere he went, his thoughts returned to the decision. "I thought about it when I was running four miles with my boots on and I knew other guys were probably working on their games," he said.

"But I did things this summer they'll never get to do. A lot of things this summer, I wouldn't trade for anything. Even some of the things I didn't like, I'm glad I did—at least once."

After his mandatory duty, David tried out for the United States squad that would play in an international tournament later in the summer in Europe. His teammates included many of the nation's top college stars—Auburn's Chuck Person, Syracuse's Rafael Addison, Virginia Tech's Dell Curry, Larry Krystkowiak of Montana and Doug Altenberger of Illinois—and they impressed him with their basketball work habits. "It was 105 degrees and these guys were busting it every day," said David. "They never wanted to stop playing. It was kind of inspiring." David, who still tended to get distracted by thoughts of a Beethoven sonata or a computer program while running up and down the hardwood, realized, "I had to keep my mind in the games and play hard myself or I'd get absolutely killed."

Unlike David, most of the players on the American squad looked at college as a training ground for the pros. All of them told him he should have transferred. But David was satisfied that he'd made the right decision.

While many people couldn't understand how a nineteen-year-old kid could possibly pass up the chance to be a millionaire, others saw him as an instant hero.

In the fall, after he returned to Annapolis to lead the Middies' air attack once again, New York Governor Mario Cuomo went on a nationally syndicated radio show.

"Occasionally there is a sports story that does not involve drugs, illegal payments, or lawsuits," he began.

"David Robinson is six-eleven and is considered by many experts to be the best center in college basketball. Usually that translates into a future multimillion dollar contract.

"But Robinson is different. He plays basketball for the Naval Academy. Last summer he had to decide whether he would stay at Navy or transfer to another college. If he stayed at Annapolis, he would be required to serve five years in the Navy. If he transferred he would almost certainly have become a multimillionaire in professional basketball.

"Considering his grades, Robinson could have gone to any college. David Robinson chose to stay at Navy. He talked about commitment, loyalty, and values. His father had been in the Navy. Annapolis offered him a free education. He said he felt an obligation to serve his country, and that money wasn't the only way of measuring happiness.

"There is considerable talk today about patriotism, loyalty, family. I wonder how many of us would choose these virtues rather than the chance of becoming a multimillionaire, especially if you were a college sophomore when you had to make that choice.

"In David Robinson we have a young man who has made that choice and who honors all of us by his willingness to place public service to his country above money and materialism."

CHAPTER V

ALL-AROUND ALL-AMERICAN

When Midshipman Second Class David Robinson returned to the Academy in the fall of 1985, he was a changed man. With his active duty requirement looming in front of him, sometimes he couldn't help but wonder whether staying at the Academy had been the right decision after all. His trip to Europe with the U.S. international squad convinced him beyond doubt that he was good enough to play pro ball. He was now over seven feet tall—and still growing. And he knew he could continue to improve his game.

He also knew that all the demands the Academy placed on his time were holding back his development. David still loved the Navy, but it was no longer the end all and be all of his existence; he now wanted to play pro ball more than anything. Basketball was his future, and he was determined to give himself the chance to become the best big man in the country and a top NBA draft choice.

At the same time, everyone was building him up,

talking about him as if he were a hero. He was just twenty years old, and was already being compared to people like Bill Bradley, the 1965 College Basketball Player of the Year who had gone on to England as a Rhodes Scholar before playing pro ball with the Knicks—and who was now a United States Senator from New Jersey. One day when he picked up *The Washington Post,* he saw an article that described him as a latter-day Thomas Merton, the American monk and author "who measured the world's offerings against a rare personal standard and went his own way."

Sure he was a good person, but a saint? He wasn't ready to give up pro ball—in fact he wanted it so badly he could almost taste it. And he wanted it as soon as possible.

From the time he got back to school, David hoped that some arrangement could be made with the Navy that would allow him to play in the NBA. He understood his responsibilities: he was at Navy to get an education; that hadn't changed. He was there to become an officer and a gentleman; that was still important too. But not least of all, he was at the Academy to play ball; the brass surely wouldn't have worked so hard to convince him to stay if they hadn't wanted him in the low post! And he concurred wholeheartedly; he couldn't wait to get back on the court with his teammates—Doug, Vernon, Kylor, Carl and the rest.

All of them were one year older, and every returning member of the team—himself included—expected the Middies to be even better than last year's NCAA tournament team. With all five starters back,

and David playing more aggressively on both ends of
the court, they felt they could play with anybody.

Of course there were still times on the court
when David's mind wandered. And when it did, he
could count on Coach Evans to start riding him, to
call him a freak of the Navy, to say that the only
reason anybody paid any attention to him was because he was tall. He knew the coach meant well, but
it was still unpleasant. He wished Evans would
lighten up.

One day a bunch of the guys were pulling in to a
Hardee's fast food restaurant. As he was getting out
of the car, David said, "Coach, look what I picked up
in Spain." He reached down, and walked across the
parking lot to the restaurant—on his hands. Everybody got a kick out of the sight of an upside-down
seven-foot Midshipman. Even the coach cracked a
smile. But in general, fun wasn't on the agenda for
David and his teammates that fall. Basketball had become a serious business.

In order to accommodate his new set of priorities, David registered that semester for what he called
a "light load": electrical engineering, weapons, history of science and technology, contemporary American literature, advanced programming, and celestial
navigation. Still, for the first time since his arrival at
the Academy, his grades suffered.

But he didn't request special treatment—not that
he would have received it had he asked. Captain Al
Konetzni, one of the top ranking officers at the Academy, said, "David cuts no slack around here. I
chewed him out just the other day for the way his
shoes looked. We work the kid hard. He's got basket-

ball. And his computers. There's just no time. On top of it all he's in love."

David had gone out with several girls since he'd been at the Academy, including some midshipman women. (Some of the other guys had given him a hard time about that, until they started seeing Navy girls themselves.) But he hadn't been serious about anybody. In the fall of his junior year, though, David started dating Stephannie Johnson, a sophomore at George Mason. He first met her a few years earlier when he was a senior at Osbourn Park and she was a cheerleader for a rival high school. She never seemed to get tired of telling people how they met, how he was going after a loose ball and ran over her on the sideline. "Watch out, you big goof," she remembered saying to him, and they laughed. Now that they were going out, he saw her as often as he could, and he called and wrote to her just about every day.

David and Stephannie had something else in common—they both wore braces. Photographers wanted pictures of the two of them smiling, and a national orthodontists' organization even interviewed them both for an article. Everybody looked at them as two All-American kids.

On some level, though, everything—school, the Navy, even Stephannie—seemed to be distractions from basketball. David could feel his growing power on the court. He could see his ability to dominate the action. And when things were going right, he could share in the Middies' tremendous ability to communicate with one another.

Six years later, Paul Evans still vividly remembered how special that Navy squad was. "It wasn't the greatest team talentwise," he said. But it was "a great team because of the chemistry. They all knew their role and they all had a lot of confidence. It was almost like a push-button team. If something wasn't working you'd make a change and that kid would do exactly what needed to be done."

David, of course, was the center of attention. But the rest of the squad's talents complemented his immense ability. "If you put the three-point line in, that team's even considerably better because Whitaker never took anything inside that line," Evans said. "So we had the good outside shooting, we had the playmaker [Wojcik] who was very unselfish, who could actually make the pass from the point into David, we had David who most teams had to double-team which left Vernon Butler, a real rugged power forward, open on the other block."

The only major problem that year was that Vernon was handicapped throughout the season from the effects of a parasitic infection. He lost thirty pounds and was not quite the banger he had been the year before. But David's increased strength more than made up for Vernon's weakness. And with Kylor switching from small forward to shooting guard, three good players (David's roommate Carl Liebert, the quick-footed freshman Nate Bailey, and Derric Turner) getting significant playing time at the small forward spot, and Cliff Rees coming off the bench to spell the starting guards, the team was both deeper and better than it had been the year before.

From the start of the season, they were also watched by the national press more closely than they ever had been before. David was constantly being interviewed, and both his and the team's performance were now scrutinized in newspapers and magazines that had ignored them a few months earlier.

The Middies also traveled just about everywhere that season—even to Japan (where they beat the pants off Army). But away from the friendly confines of Halsey they also lost three of their first ten games to nationally ranked teams. In the season opener, despite David's 27 points and 18 rebounds, Walter Berry, Mark Jackson, and St. John's beat the Middies in the Big Apple NIT. Then, after four relatively easy games, they went into the Carrier Dome to play Syracuse. It was no contest; playing in front of the Orangemen's 20,000-strong home crowd with Big East refs, Navy got blown out. After beating Air Force and Army, the Middies traveled down to Atlanta, where they had been invited to play in the Cotton States Classic. They defeated DePaul, then went up against another home team: ACC power Georgia Tech. With the Yellow Jackets' 7' center, John Salley, leaning on him all game, David was held to just 7 rebounds. Their forward Tom Hammonds was also tough down low. And in the end, with Tech guard Mark Price leading the offense, the home team had too much firepower for Navy to contend with.

Despite the losses, David was better than ever. He was more aggressive on both ends of the court, driving to the hoop, looking for his shots, and jumping out to block shots on defense. And he knew he could do even better. "I can improve," he confidently told *The Sporting News*. "There have been things going wrong. I have been losing my concentration sometimes, like a lull for five minutes where I don't

do anything. I don't feel like I'm doing my job. That
has been happening too much."

Privately, Coach Evans agreed with David's self-
assessment. He pushed him to concentrate harder, to
keep himself in the game for forty minutes. In public,
though, the coach minimized David's self-criticism as
a case of perfectionism gone too far: "David can find
fault when he shoots twelve for twelve."

□

After coming back from Atlanta with a seven and
three record, the Middies knew they had to buckle
down for their conference schedule. But with all the
traveling, they also knew they'd better buckle down
and study.

David was used to the usual demands on his time
—eighteen hours of classes, homework, formations,
military training, and the rest—and he'd shown that
he could handle practice and games. But all the fre-
quent flyer miles and all the attention finally began to
affect him.

Carl Liebert sometimes half-complained about
how easy everything seemed for his roommate. The
6-7 Hoosier from Floyds Knob said, "I have to study
hard for my grades. But David doesn't. He'll read a
book in one night and be ready for his tests." But that
wasn't completely accurate, not now anyway.

David prided himself on his academic achieve-
ments, but there simply wasn't enough time in the
day for him to study and devote as much energy to
basketball as it required. He couldn't juggle everything—and with basketball taking center stage, his
schoolwork suffered. One time, the math whiz even

failed a math test; he was depressed for days thereafter. And even though he knew he wanted to play in the NBA, he was distressed in general about his plummeting grade point average, which at the end of the first semester had fallen all the way to a 2.4. He knew he'd have to work harder.

One night early in the spring semester, after a one-man show by David on the road in Delaware (he single-handedly overwhelmed the home team with a 37-point, 14-rebound performance), the Middies got off the bus and went back to their rooms in Bancroft Hall. It was late, and Carl immediately started getting ready for sleep. David, on the other hand, came in and went straight to his computer. He had an assignment due the next morning for his advanced programming class—and when reveille woke Carl up, he discovered that his roommate had pulled an all-nighter.

Carl had been friends with David since they were plebes. He'd seen the way his roommate's talent had transformed his life and his dreams about the future. When they'd arrived at the Academy two and a half years earlier, his friend wasn't much taller than he was and basketball was nothing more than a hobby. But since Induction Day, Carl noticed that David's "feet kept hanging farther and farther over the end of the bed." Dave's hanging feet had changed a lot of things in his life; being that tall—and that good a ballplayer—had certainly changed his perspective. Now, when David and Carl talked about their plans —after the Academy—Carl's "wish list" was pretty standard for a midshipman, but Dave's was very different. It was no secret that he hoped something could be done to delay, defer, or limit his service obligation. Dave wanted to play basketball when he graduated.

□

Throughout the year, David also continued to have the full support of his family: his dad still came up on Saturday mornings, and the whole family remained fanatical Navy hoops fans. When a game was too far away for Ambrose to get to, and it wasn't on TV, he would drive the white Bonneville up from Dale City to Telegraph Road in Alexandria, where he would be close enough to Annapolis to pick up the play-by-play on the radio. Ambrose would pull off the road, park the car in an empty lot, and listen. During the Delaware game, a police officer came up to his car and asked to see his ID. "I'm listening to the basketball game," Ambrose explained. "My son plays for Navy." When the officer saw the name on the license, he said hello, wished him luck, and went his own way.

Ambrose made videotapes of the games, and painstakingly pieced together his son's slam-dunk highlights. According to Paul Evans, he was "the perfect parent as far as a coach is concerned. He never had any advice or anything he didn't like. He was very easy to get along with. You were happy to see him show up because it boosted David's spirits and got him working a little bit harder."

David's mother was also at Halsey for home games, shouting encouragement to her son from the opening tap to the final buzzer. And his brother Chuckie, a high school freshman, had an incurable case of hero worship when it came to his big brother. Chuck was doing virtually everything he could to follow in David's footsteps—he played basketball at Osbourn Park (and was actually taller than David had been at the same age), and like his brother, he wanted to grow up and study engineering. But he wasn't so sure about following his brother to the Academy—"I don't think I could handle being told what to do all the time," he said.

□

By the end of the regular season, Navy lost only one more game, to a strong Richmond team before a standing-room only crowd on the Spiders' home court. But even that loss was mitigated by an easy victory over Richmond in the final game of the campaign back at Halsey.

The Middies had only one other close call. In their next to the last game of the regular season, they went up to West Point to play Army and nearly got ambushed. The Cadets' physical play stifled David from the opening minute, and held him to just 2 points in the entire first half. He scored 14 after the intermission as Navy came back to force an overtime. Finally, David took over in the extra session, scoring 7 of his team's 11 points and leading the Middies to a narrow 55-52 escape.

Navy finished the regular season with a 24 and 4 record that included a season-ending ten game winning streak and seventeen victories in their last eighteen games. But they couldn't rest on their laurels; other challenges lay ahead.

Coach Evans reminded the team that there'd

never been two CAA squads to make the NCAA field in the same year, and that despite their superb record, the Middies had to do well in the conference tournament to assure themselves a bid. He drove the team hard in practice, prodding David in particular, trying to goad him into greater intensity and focus on the court. When his center appeared to be walking lackadaisically through practice, the coach exploded and kicked him off the court.

Coach Evans often used the tension between himself and his star player to motivate the laid-back Middie, figuring that once David got angry at him, he would take it out on the other team. It was a useful strategy. "I would block him out," David said, "but the fact that he was yelling at me would make me mad and start me up."

In the Colonial Tournament, Navy had no problem in the opening round against a weak James Madison squad, but they barely survived the semis, beating UNC-Wilmington by just two points, despite Midshipman Robinson's heroics. After David dominated the boards and led all Navy scorers in carrying the Middies over his team, UNC-Wilmington coach Mel Gibson marveled, "On one of those tips he came in from about thirteen feet. That's an airplane flying up there."

In the final, George Mason tried to shoot down the Navy's air force by hacking him into submission, but even though David was horrendous from the line, shooting just ten for eighteen, he led the Middies to an easy 72-61 victory.

With 80 points and 47 rebounds in three games, David was easily selected tournament MVP. And when Colonial Athletic Association Commissioner Tom Yeager presented him with the award for the conference Player of the Year, he also acknowledged the overall talent of the league's best player: "We are all proud that it took him over two and a half years to score more points on the court than on his SAT."

David scored in double figures in every one of Navy's thirty-one games. He was the leading rebounder in the country, and was also the only player in the nation to average more than 20 points and 10 rebounds and shoot better than 60 percent from the floor for the season. He was just as effective on the defensive end, having proved himself to be far and away the most devastating shot blocker in the college game. His all-around talent was exemplified by three remarkable triple-doubles—in which he hit double figures in points, rebounds, and blocks. In one of those games, against UNC-Wilmington, he'd also broken the all-time NCAA record for most blocks in a game, with 14.

Midshipman David Robinson was selected as a first team All-American by *The Sporting News,* the *Los Angeles Times, Eastern Basketball,* and ESPN. The US Basketball Writers Association and the National Association of Basketball Coaches both named him to their second team, and UPI, AP, and *Basketball Weekly* (voting before the beginning of post-season play), named him as a third team All-American.

By the middle of March David was sitting on top of the college basketball world. But there was still one more mountain to climb—the NCAAs.

□

When the seedings for the tournament were announced, it felt like a slap in the face to Navy. What
more could they have done to gain the respect of the
NCAA seeding committee? They'd come out on top
in thirteen straight games, and all four teams they'd
lost to were in the tournament field (three were
seeded either first or second in their regionals). Still,
the Middies were seeded seventh in the East, which
meant that the selection committee considered at
least twenty-four teams to be superior to them. The
emotional Evans was in a rage: "They dumped on us
again," he fumed. Midshipmen Robinson and Butler
also made no bones about their disappointment at
their placement, but they had no recourse; the Middies set out to win the respect they deserved on the
court.

Navy found itself in a subregional in the Carrier
Dome in Syracuse. They had to get past Tulsa, the
Missouri Valley champ, in the first round. After that,
they'd almost certainly have to play Syracuse—on the
Orangemen's home court. Judging by the 22-point
loss they'd suffered to Syracuse early in the regular
season, they didn't seem to have much of a chance.
But they knew if they worried too much about their
second round matchup, they might just get blown
away by Tulsa's Golden Hurricane.

The Middies battened down the hatches and
came out with a storm front of their own. Tenth-
seeded Tulsa may have been the fifth best defensive
team in the country, but in the first half Navy's powerful big-man tandem made mincemeat of them in-

side. Between them, David and Vernon Butler scored 31 points before the intermission, wearing down the Oklahomans and setting the stage for a second-half blowout. In the end, David finished with 30 points, 12 rebounds, and 5 blocks, Vernon added 25 points and 11 boards, and Navy's backcourt duo of Whitaker and Wojcik combined for 19 assists. It was time for a rematch with the Orangemen.

On the night of March 16th David Robinson and the Middies forced the entire nation to take them seriously. With little more than six minutes gone, it was all Syracuse. The Orangemen had already racked up a 15-7 lead, with Pearl Washington effortlessly penetrating and dissecting the Navy zone. Evans had to adjust or abandon ship. He called timeout, took Carl Liebert out of the game and replaced him with the quick 6-6 plebe Nathan Bailey. The coach also moved David from the right side of the 2-3 zone to the center, where he hoped the seven-footer's long arms and quickness would cut off Washington's passing lanes.

With David asserting himself at both ends of the court, the Middies immediately started getting back in the game. As the Navy center turned on his power, his highly touted counterpart, Rony Seikaly, turned invisible.

The Navy guards started to loft the ball inside for alley-oop slams, and Seikaly and his teammates were forced to foul David to keep him away from the glass. When David was double-teamed, Vernon exploited the weak side for easy layups.

But it was on the other end of the floor that the game turned. David Robinson was *the force*—he intimidated any Orangeman who dared stray into his neighborhood, preventing passes inside, blocking shots, and creating general havoc.

Early in the second half, with Syracuse holding a 39-37 lead, Navy's aircraft carrier took charge. When the Orangemen tried to penetrate, David's long arms seemed to be everywhere. Unable to go inside, they forced shots up from the perimeter—and missed. In one remarkable sequence, David blocked a shot to start a fast break, loped downcourt, and with his electrifying long strides, sped past the Syracuse defense and appeared suddenly at the other end in perfect position to add an exclamation point to the fast break by slamming in a teammate's miss for a deuce.

When Seikaly fouled out with 7:11 remaining, he had only 4 points, 4 rebounds and 3 blocked shots. Forty-five seconds later, Navy had a 17-point lead. The game was over.

The stunned crowd filed quietly out of the huge arena. Pearl Washington declared, "I consider Robinson the best player in the country. He's in a class with Patrick Ewing. He's the franchise." A dejected Jim Boeheim agreed. "He was the difference," said the Syracuse coach. "Without him, they can't beat anybody in the country."

On the other side of the court Paul Evans felt vindicated and couldn't resist the desire to gloat. "Not too bad for a bunch of short hairs," he mused.

David Robinson finished with 35 points, 11 rebounds and 7 blocked shots, and converted a remarkable 21 for 27 from the foul line. There were only sixteen teams left in the tournament, and Navy was one of them.

The next week in the Meadowlands, the Midshipmen were matched up in the East regional semis against no-name Cleveland State, an even bigger dark horse than the Middies themselves. On the way to the third-round showdown, the Vikings' colorful Boston-Irish coach, Kevin Mackey, had upset Professor Bob Knight's Indiana Hoosiers with an all-out, forty-minute, baseline-to-baseline attack. Mackey, in his inimitable style, billed the Meadowlands matchup "The U.S. Navy Department of Defense against the U.S. Stun and Gun, Streetfighters Inc."

It was indeed a street fight . . . and it went right down to the wire. For most of the game, David was a nonfactor. He picked up three fouls in the first half, but was picked up by his teammates, particularly Kylor Whitaker, who shot well, passed smartly, and refused to be rattled by Cleveland State's in-your-face style.

But in the second half, with the Vikings bumping and grinding all over the court, David and the rest of the Middies grew increasingly frustrated. It seemed as if the player in Navy uniform number 50 was an impostor; it couldn't possibly be the same man who had dominated Syracuse. As the minutes passed, Navy's aircraft carrier never even seemed to see the ball. Finally, the underdog Vikings surged into the lead with nine minutes left.

The Meadowlands crowd, including 600 midshipmen and Admiral James Watkins, the Chief of Naval Operations, couldn't believe their eyes. Neither could Paul Evans.

Evans was an emotional coach who was not afraid to say exactly what he thought. He called a timeout, and told his players, "You're going to kick this away doing it your way."

He then turned to David and, with fire in his eyes, urged him to fight for the ball and take it to the hole at every opportunity. Evans' words had their desired effect—Navy's sleeping giant awoke with a fury.

In the last six minutes David became a one-man gang. He scored 12 of the Middies' last 14 points, hitting jumpers, free throws, and dunks. He controlled the glass and swatted away shots like they were flies. In the end, Navy's "Sultan of Smooth" scuttled the Vikings' hopes. He finished with 22 points (including the winning bucket with six seconds left), grabbed 14 rebounds, and blocked 9 shots. Afterwards, Evans said "he looked like a man playing with boys."

The NBA scouts, meanwhile, were eating their hearts out. They saw a player who had everything—size, athleticism, intelligence, and extraordinary speed. "Why am I torturing myself?" one scout reportedly moaned. Marty Blake, the NBA's most influential evaulator of talent, declared that David was the league's certain number one draft pick after his senior year—if he was available. And Bob Ferry of the Bullets, when asked if Midshipman Robinson had any shortcomings as a pro, replied, "Yeah, he's in the Navy."

In three tournament games, one of the nation's best kept secrets was revealed: David had proven to everyone that he was the best big man in the college ranks, a prospect on a par with Ewing and Olajuwon.

He also proved to himself that he could play with anybody. "I know what I'm capable of," he said confidently. David openly predicted that he would control the paint against Navy's next opponent, a smaller Duke squad that also happened to be the top-ranked team in the country. And at first he did.

He scored Navy's first 7 points, and with just over seven minutes left in the first half, David was leading a new charge on both ends of the floor. Suddenly, though, the tide turned, and the Middies' 20-16 lead evaporated in the face of a brigade of Blue Devils. Navy's big man was double- and triple-teamed, boxed out and bullied by waves of Blue Devils, including Jay Bilas, Mark Alarie, and Danny Ferry. The Middies were massacred under the boards, and by halftime, Duke had scored 18 of the period's last 20 points. David finished the first half with good numbers—15 points and 7 rebounds—but Duke held a 34-22 lead.

In the second half, the Blue Devils continued their dominance inside. With eleven minutes left and the lead standing at 54-31, the Duke cheering section started shouting at the Middies to abandon ship. When it was over, Navy had been literally blown out of the water. There was no question as to who was better—on their way to a 71-50 victory, Duke outrebounded the Middies by an amazing 49-29 margin.

David was angry, dejected, even humiliated. "I didn't expect to get killed on the boards," he said. "We played like girls inside."

□

Despite the disappointing end to the Middies' season, it had been the greatest year in Navy basketball history. The team finished with a record of 30-5, and reached the Final Eight of the NCAA tournament.

As for Navy's rising star, by season's end he had become the most dominating center in the country, a player whose ability and potential seemed to have no limits. He was among the nation's leaders in scoring, shooting percentage, and rebounding. And, most remarkably, he blocked more shots than any *team* in the country except Louisville, the squad that finally beat Duke for the national championship. (The Cardinals, however, needed 39 games to finish with 213 blocks; David got his 207 in just 35.)

He had done it all. What could he do for an encore?

CHAPTER VI

SENIOR SUMMER

In large part Midshipman David Robinson's senior summer could be summed up in a few choice phrases: "Join the Navy . . . play some ball . . . stand your ground . . . and see the world!"

David was following the case of Ensign Napoleon McCallum very closely (Nap, an All-American running back at the Academy, had been given permission by the Navy to serve as a commissioned officer during the week and play pro football with the Los Angeles Raiders on weekends). He was hoping that McCallum would be successful at his double duty; if Nap could pull it off he would prove to the brass that an officer can play professional sports while honoring his commission. But David was too busy with his own double duty to dwell at length on all the uncertainties in his life.

When the Academy sent the rest of its resident midshipmen on their summer cruises, David was released from his assignment in time to arrive in Colorado City, where a convocation of coaches was convening with the sole purpose of picking a squad to

represent the United States in the World Basketball
Championships in July. There was little time to
choose, much less to prepare a team, so the American
head coach, Arizona's Lute Olson, ordered the players to get an early start in the morning. Olson gave
Arizona student manager Nick Bougopoulos the
unenviable job of waking them each morning at six.
He told the *Arizona Daily Star* that when he arrived
shortly after dawn, Robinson was invariably "already
up brushing his teeth. Everyone else was in bed."
David told Bougopoulos that the schedule was routine at the Academy.

It was a tough tryout camp for both the prospec-
tive team members and the U.S. coaching staff, and it
became even tougher when many of their top
frontcourt prospects started to fall by the wayside. A
number of big men, including college player of the
year Walter Berry, entered the NBA draft as under-
graduates. The Kansas Jayhawks' sophomore star,
Danny Manning, left camp early because of an injury,
and Louisville's shot-blocking sensation Pervis Elli-
son was sent packing after missing a practice. After
his spectacular performance in the NCAAs, David
presumably would have made the national team if he
had walked through the trials. But if he expected to
be successful in international competition, he needed
to do more than just make the team; he had to learn a
whole new style of play. David was undoubtedly the
U.S.A.'s best big man and America's only real hope
of withstanding the tough and experienced international centers, most notably the Soviet Union's 7-2
superstar, Arvidas Sabonis. To earn the gold, he first

had to play hard, and work hard, at the trials in Colorado Springs.

After the tryouts were completed, most of those chosen for the team had three weeks off (presumably to catch up on their sleep). And while coach Lute Olson prepared for the upcoming world championships with a little R & R in Hawaii that June, his starting center was also in the islands . . . serving a three-week tour of duty on an aircraft carrier and a submarine.

Although David got off the sub at the end of his mandatory cruise, he didn't come up for air. As soon as Midshipman Robinson regained his land legs, he joined the United States team back on the mainland for a series of two-a-day practices in the sweltering summer heat of Tucson. There, Olson and his staff put the players through a two-week crash course in international basketball, and did their best to teach their starting center the rudiments of a man-to-man defense (which he had *never* played). Olson was also concerned about David's offense. While the coaches were drilling the team in practice—going high-post, low-post, pass and pick away—at times David seemed utterly lost. He simply didn't know the subtleties of the game. But he was learning, and on raw talent alone, he was still the best center Lute Olson had.

After training camp, it was on to France, where the Americans got their feet wet in international competition with a few exhibition games against European teams.

The players were pretty set in their ways; basketball was the center of their lives, whether they were in the States or in Europe. And each of them was singleminded in his pursuit of the dream of a pro basketball career.

David traveled on the same bus as the rest of the team, but sometimes he appeared to be on his own trip. "I'll never forget one time," remembered Bobby Cremins, the Georgia Tech coach who was one of Olson's assistants that summer, "we were on the side of the road in France. I asked David, who sometimes played hard and sometimes didn't, why he didn't always play hard. He said, 'Coach, basketball is not a big part of my life. It's just not that important to me. I've already got a career in the Navy.'"

Cremins couldn't get over David's wide range of interests. Still, the coach thought, America's star center needed to be focused on the task at hand if he ever hoped to reach his potential. David agreed. He told Cremins that, with the NBA's big money obviously in his future, he was beginning to become more motivated, but that it would take a little more time to get used to the idea of basketball as more than just one more facet of his life.

After finishing the exhibition tour, the team moved on to Malaga, Spain, for the first round of the World Championships. The U.S. team in Malaga was billeted in a hotel surrounded by local police. With the ever-present threat of international terrorism against Americans in Europe that summer, it was not unusual for the players to see uniformed men, armed with automatic weapons, on the roof of the hotel. Nor was it surprising (although it was distracting) for the team to be transported to and from games in a bus with a police motorcycle escort. While David (with his Navy background) could talk to his team-mates about military preparedness and deterrent force, another American player, Arizona's Steve Kerr, knew about terrorism first-hand: his father had been serving as president of the American University in Beirut when he was assassinated in 1984.

Coming into the competition, the U.S. squad put the threat of terrorism out of their minds and began to concentrate on winning. In their first two games, they sailed past the Ivory Coast (whose rooting section drummed and snake-danced their way through the arena), and China (whose coach, when asked how soon his country would be competitive with the United States in basketball, replied "As soon as you are competitive with China in Ping-Pong.") The young Americans (average age twenty) finally came up against some real competition in a tough, experienced West German squad. And for the first time in the tournament, David was a leader. Charles Smith of Pitt led the way in scoring, with 23, and Kenny Smith of North Carolina added 13 (including three uncontested layups off steals), but David asserted himself off the boards, hitting 7 of 9 from the floor for 16 points and controlling the glass during a crucial run early in the second half when the U.S. broke the game open.

In their next game, despite sloppy play in the last minute, the U.S. lucked out when Puerto Rico's Mario Morales (who had stolen the ball from Kenny Smith) missed a layup at the buzzer, thus allowing a jumper by America's big man to hold up as the winning bucket.

International basketball is a physical game,

played with a lot less finesse and a lot more banging than American college ball. The whistles, when they occur, often seem to have little rhyme or reason for those used to American NCAA-style officiating. David had played in an international tournament the year before, and his game had been considered a little soft. He was, after all, "the Sultan of Smooth." But with a showdown against the 7-2, 250-pound Soviet behemoth Sabonis looming on the horizon, he had advanced light-years in toughness from last year.

After an unexpectedly easy and impressive victory over Italy, in which David had 14 points, 10 rebounds, and 6 blocks, he commented, "There's been no fighting. But there have been times when I've been jolted, seen stars for a second." The wiry Midshipman was proving to himself that he could stand his ground against opposition roughhouse tactics; he refused to be intimidated.

Although the young Americans finished their preliminary round undefeated, the general consensus in Malaga was that the two top teams were the Soviet Union and Yugoslavia. The Europeans, to a man, were still writing the United States off as too young, too inexperienced, and not physical enough. But the Americans had come to win, and despite their youth they were confident that they could play with anyone. It wouldn't be easy, though. And David, in particular, knew that the chances for a U.S. victory depended in large part on him, especially in a matchup with the Soviets, where his ability to stay with Sabonis would be crucial for success.

□

The Americans came out flat in the first semifinal game, losing to Argentina, 74-70. David had 13 points, but shot just 4-12 from the floor. But the defeat couldn't be blamed on any one player; it was a team effort all the way. The Americans were totally uninspired, passing the ball poorly (they accumulated a total of two assists for the game) and shooting just as badly (they hit less than 50 percent from the foul line).

If the Yanks were to have even a chance to win the gold, and if their showdown with the Soviet Union was to mean anything, they would first have to beat both Canada and Yugoslavia to qualify for the medal round.

After taking care of the Canadians, the young Americans came up against their counterparts from Yugoslavia, led by the flashy 6-6 guard Drazen Petrovic. Petro was hounded by the diminutive Tyrone "Muggsy" Bogues, and before the Yugoslavs could collect themselves, they were behind 19-2. From there it was a cakewalk, and at the final buzzer, the score was 69-60. The United States, Yugoslavia, Brazil, and the U.S.S.R. were the final four.

In the semis, the U.S. faced Brazil and the Soviets came up against the Yugoslavs. The Americans, utilizing a pressing, opportunistic man-to-man defense, a devastating fast break, and a balanced scoring attack, tore into the Brazilians early, taking a 50-24 lead with five minutes left in the first half. But Brazil fought back. With their legendary high scoring guard Oscar Schmidt bombing away from the outside, they cut the lead to 60-47 by the time six and a half minutes had elapsed in the second half. The

U.S., meanwhile, which had cut through the Brazilian defense to score at will in the first half, stopped doing everything that had made their offense so effective earlier. They stood around, didn't move the ball, and started throwing up bricks. While the Brazilians piled up the points, the stone-cold Americans had a big goose egg. Finally, a third of the way into the period, David broke the drought with a clutch bucket, and the Americans began to regain some of their lost poise. But the Brazilians weren't quite done with their run. Schmidt continued his brilliant shooting and they kept whittling away at the lead, finally cutting the margin to nine with 6:44 left. But they had fallen too far behind to come all the way back, and they simply ran out of gas as the U.S. ran away to a 96-80 victory. David led six Yanks in double figures with 17 points. And the surprising Americans were in the final.

Olson's young players had overcome their inexperience and come through. Their quickness, court fundamentals, and youthful enthusiasm enabled them to go much farther than anyone expected. "If someone would have told me two weeks ago we would be within one game of the world championship, I would have said, 'You're loco,'" said the happy American coach.

In the championship game, the U.S. college kids faced the tough, experienced Soviets. (The Russians had qualified with a miracle finish, erasing a 9-point Yugoslav lead with less than a minute to remain in regulation and holding on to eke out a one-point—91-90—overtime triumph.) America's chances against the Russians rested on their all-court quickness, and on the ability of Navy's tall ship, Midshipman David Robinson (with only four years of competitive experience *at any level*), to neutralize the brute strength and skills of the U.S.S.R.'s giant center Sabonis.

From the first minute David showed he was a force to be reckoned with. Within seconds of the opening tip, he controlled the offensive board and put in a follow. He refused to be intimidated, and throughout the first half made Sabonis seem a half-step slow. With Robinson scoring 17 points by intermission, and Wake Forest's 5-3 Muggsy Bogues driving the Russian guards crazy (he finished with 10 steals) the U.S. left the floor with a 10-point lead. A strong second half by Kenny Smith increased the margin to 78-60 with under eight minutes left. Then the Soviets got their wake-up call. Determined to duplicate their miracle finish against the Yugoslavs, they came back, and with Sabonis dominating the paint, they whittled the lead down, minute after excruciating minute. Two rim-rattling Sabonis slams brought the Soviets to within eight with 4:41 left. The exhausted Americans stopped playing with confidence and began to watch the clock. David, in particular, reeled under the onslaught. The game seemed to go on forever. "I didn't think it would ever end," he said later.

With fifteen seconds left and the U.S. holding an 85-83 lead, Kenny Smith drove down the lane. Twice before he had penetrated and dished off when Sabonis picked him up. This time the Soviet bear hesitated, and Smith went by him to lay it in. Five seconds later, the Soviets' Sergei Taraknov answered with a drive, bringing the Russians back to 87-85. The U.S. lost the ball off the inbounds pass, but the Soviet Union's smooth point guard Valdis Valters missed a shot at the buzzer. For the first time since 1954, the United States won the World Basketball Championships.

It had been a cram course in competition for the young U.S. team—especially for the man in the middle. For the first time, David had to go one-on-one with world-class athletes his own size, without the protection that Paul Evans' 2-3 zone provided for his still-raw defensive skills. David had always been able to float across the Navy zone without being leaned on. Despite his awesome shot-blocking during the college season, he had never before been forced to guard a tough, physical low-post operator without help. And he'd never had to play against anyone with Sabonis' world-class combination of size and skills.

David held his own throughout the games, averaging over 13 points, almost 7 rebounds, and 2 1/2 blocks. And he saved his best game for last, outscoring international basketball's most dominating center. But most important of all, he loved the experience, and it made him think about just how central basketball had become in his life. He never wanted to live without hoops again.

CHAPTER VII

PLAYER OF THE YEAR

When David returned to Annapolis in the fall of 1986, he was more clearly focused than ever on basketball. His experience in the previous spring's NCAA tournament, plus his performance in the world championships against Sabonis, convinced him beyond a shadow of a doubt that he had finally found something he could be the best at. He really could have a future in this game.

David's recognition of his own potential lit a fire under him, and gave him the impetus to become a student of the game. For the first time, he seriously started watching tapes. He studied Kareem Abdul-Jabbar's unstoppable skyhook and Kevin McHale's uncanny ability to rebound without getting off the ground, and he began to use his keen intelligence to analyze the game's great players, trying to find the keys to their success. And he did it all with the idea that he would someday join them at the top.

He also knew that he had to rely on himself for motivation because his chief outside agitator—the coach whose incessant prodding had pushed him into realizing his potential—was gone.

The previous year, Paul Evans had been offered other jobs, but he turned them down; if he were to leave Navy, he reasoned, it would be to go to a school with a nationally prominent program. He had, in fact, applied for the vacancy at Kentucky, but was passed over in favor of one of coaching's household names, Eddie Sutton.

Although Evans was a strict disciplinarian with his players, he made no bones about not being the Navy type—he joked that he couldn't think of anything worse than getting up before dawn (as his players did all winter). And while he was proud of his "short hairs," he wanted the opportunity to recruit blue-chip athletes and compete in one of the big time conferences.

In 1986 there was no conference in the country with a better recent track record than the Big East. Georgetown won the national championship in '84; and in '85, when Villanova's "perfect game" dethroned the Hoyas, an unprecedented three of the Final Four teams came from the Big East. Thus, when Evans was offered the head coaching position at the University of Pittsburgh, he knew he would be joining the league of John Thompson, Rollie Massimino, Louie Carnesecca, and Jim Boeheim—he'd be at the very top of his profession.

But there was another reason why Evans wanted to leave in the spring of '86: "I didn't want to ride out David and have people say he stayed as long as David was here and then left," as though abandoning a sinking ship.

Even though his gut feeling was that it was time to move on, Evans felt he first owed David an explanation and a discussion of the young star's plans. He didn't forget that Midshipman Robinson had stayed on the team after his freshman year, when the coach told him he thought he had the potential to be a pro. Nor could he ignore David's decision after his sophomore year, when staying at Navy required a deep commitment and meant a huge sacrifice. Evans felt he owed the same loyalty to David that his young center had shown to him and the program.

"I talked to Ambrose and David and told them it was a situation I thought I liked but that I didn't want to leave if they thought I was jeopardizing him," Evans said. Both Ambrose and David said, 'No, Coach.' " Evans had already decided that if the Robinsons asked him to stay, he would pass up the Pitt job. But they didn't stand in his way.

Evans discussed his plans with the Navy athletic brass, and urged them to keep his system intact for David's senior year. "If they'd gone outside, it could have really hurt him," Evans said. "If some guy came in with a motion offense or something completely unfamiliar to David, then his stock would have gone down." The athletic department wholeheartedly agreed with Evans's recommendation, and when he accepted the job at Pitt, his assistant Pete Herrmann replaced him, "because we knew he wouldn't change the system for [David's] senior year."

Still, when the Middies returned to Halsey for preseason practice, David was the only Navy player who had averaged more than 5.3 points per game in the previous season. Doug Wojcik was back, as was

Carl Liebert, but the two top members of his supporting cast, Vernon Butler and Kylor Whitaker, had
both graduated to become commissioned officers in
the Navy.

For the first time, David was also seriously disaf-
fected with the Naval Academy. Although he tried to
dismiss his feelings as "senioritis," it was becoming
increasingly hard to justify the decision he had made
a year and a half earlier. "I have to put out so much
effort in the Navy that it detracts from my basketball," he said. "If I wanted to go out and shoot free
throws during study hours, I couldn't do it. It's built
into the system. Everyone has to do the same stuff,
no matter who you are. You have to be there for
formations, have to go to class. A lot of the things are
a pain to do, but nobody's excluded from them."

He spoke openly about his second thoughts to
The Washington Post: "If I had known two years ago
that I would feel this way now, I probably would
have made a different decision and not stayed here. I
came here because I wanted to be in the Navy. That
was what I cared about. But I've changed.

"The irony is if I hadn't come here I might never
have found out what kind of player I could be, I
might not have had a chance to become this good.
Now I want the chance to get better."

Paul Evans later said, "Most definitely if he went
in [to the ACC] in his freshman year, I don't think
you would have seen David play four years of basketball." David concurred; he knew he would have been
overwhelmed by the competition had he gone to a
big-time basketball school as a freshman.

His strong desire to play pro ball made the me-

dia's insistence on portraying him as a hero some-
what ludicrous. "I don't see myself like that at all,"
he declared. "I'm a good person but sorry, I'm not a
traditional American hero." On the other hand, he
reasoned, "It's better than having a bad reputation."

As if the Navy wasn't distracting enough, he was
now just about everybody's preseason pick as the college player of the year. All the attention was flatter-
ing, but it also consumed almost all his remaining
"free" time. Every day some reporter wanted to interview him and a photographer wanted to shoot his
picture. *Sports Illustrated* asked him to pose for the
cover of their college hoops issue, and they flew him
to Norfolk to stand at attention in his dress whites in
front of the U.S.S. *Iowa*. It was a terrific picture and
a real ego-boosting article, but it too had its down-
side, causing hassles later with the NCAA, which
questioned the Academy about how much expense
money the magazine had given him.

There were days, even whole weeks when David
didn't seem to have a minute to relax. It was a big
adjustment, and it looked like there would be no end
to it. Finally, to keep things from getting out of control, David limited his interviews to one day a week.

Whenever he had a chance—between basketball,
interviews, advanced numerical analysis, computer
data structures, partial differential equations, eco-
nomic geography, formations, drills, watch, Regi-
mental Supply Officer duties (overseeing distribution
of everyday living supplies to 2,700 Midshipmen),
charity work, and the rest of his obligations—David
tried to give himself the time and space he needed.
He was known in the yard for blasting his stereo

throughout his company's wing of Bancroft Hall. And when he could, he'd sit down at a piano and figure out something he could play by ear, generally a new song by Sting or some other avant-jazz pop-rocker. (Not that he'd given up Beethoven.)

In some ways he still felt close to his teammates, but he also knew his life was diverging from theirs. It wasn't just that he was looking ahead—beyond his Naval commitment—to becoming a millionaire pro ballplayer, while they had their sights set on careers as officers. He also felt deeply disappointed and hurt at not being chosen captain of the team. On the court, nobody could dispute that he was Navy's main man. And he'd always thought the other players respected him, that they were his friends. So when the Middie players selected Doug Wojcik as their leader, David felt slighted, and his family wondered whether there might not be a racial component to their decision.

David also later spoke about the "little areas of friction" on the team, the "jealousy." He felt some of the other players resented his success, and that, "as Navy emerged as a team, something other than just fun came with it."

Whatever happened with his coach and his teammates, Navy's star was still his own man; he'd always march to a different drummer. "Dave is not a coach's player, not one of those gung-ho guys," said the new head coach, Pete Herrmann. "It's not in his personality. His nature is laid back. But in big games, there's nobody I'd rather have on my team."

The first big game came in the season opener, against Jim Valvano's North Carolina State Wolfpack.

Before the encounter, Valvano heaped praise on David, saying, "Robinson is different than the other great big men we've faced like Sampson and Olajuwon. He runs the floor and dunks on follow shots. He doesn't shoot like Hakeem does, but he's so quick to the basket it's frightening."

Against the Wolfpack, David showed that he was even better than he'd been the year before. He turned on the power in the second half after Navy fell behind by 16. In a remarkable nine and a half minutes of sheer domination, he scored 20 points, and single-handedly brought the Middies back with a spectacular array of rebounds, blocks, fast break finishes, turnaround jump shots, and rim-rattling slam dunks. But his team lost 86-84.

After the game, North Carolina State's Bennie Bolton said, "He's got my vote for National Player of the Year right now. We tried everything on him. We pushed him, shoved him, tried to beat him up . . . We couldn't stop him."

Despite the praise, when David went into the silent, disappointed Middie locker room he apologized to his teammates for letting them down. He had played poorly in the first half (scoring just 10 and playing passively on defense), and had fouled out with 1:23 left and his team holding a slim one-point lead. "Good players help their teams win," he said. "All the points in the world don't matter if you lose."

The next week, against Big Ten power Michigan State, David got his points and Navy won. He controlled the game from the opening tip. It was apparent, though, that this year's supporting cast would not be able to pick up the scoring slack the way

Vernon and Kylor had done. Each victory against strong competition would depend more than ever on David keeping his head in the game from start to finish. Against the Spartans, he scored a career-high 43 points, but it wasn't until his last bucket, in the final seconds of overtime, that Navy was assured of a happy ending. This time they won the cliffhanger, 91-90.

During the Christmas break, the Middies traveled to Las Vegas where they were the guests of UNLV in the Runnin' Rebel Classic. David had never seen anything like Vegas before—he was impressed by the flash and dash of the city, its lavish hotels and neon casinos, UNLV's massive and modern Thomas & Mack Center, the pregame ceremonies (with multicolored spotlights, exciting music, and the literal red carpet treatment for the home team), and of course, with the Rebels themselves. He could hardly believe that the UNLV players could remain focused in such an atmosphere.

It was a tough tournament. After Navy beat Idaho State in their opener, they were never in the game against UNLV. The Rebs seemed to be able to run at will, and despite David's 29 points, the Middies got blown out by Jerry Tarkanian's nationally ranked powerhouse, 104-79.

The Navy squad returned to Annapolis, where their star spent the first week of the New Year worried, distracted, and uncertain about his future. The Navy had made certain assurances to him and his family when he remained at the Academy after his sophomore year, but now he didn't know whether they'd stand by their agreements. Any day now he knew his status would finally be clarified. He was hoping they'd tell him he could play pro ball right after graduation, as they had allowed Napoleon McCallum to do in the fall. But he was scared that instead he'd be ordered to fulfill the full five-year commitment. Uncertainty was the worst part—sometimes he felt that finding out where he stood, whatever the decision, would be better than not knowing.

In the Middies' next game, against North Carolina-Wilmington and their fine center Brian Rowsom, David was far from his best. The Seahawks double-teamed him almost every time he touched the ball, and he scored just 12 points before fouling out. Two nights later, though, despite the ever-increasing pressure, he came back strong against East Carolina, scoring 31 points in a convincing victory.

Next came the worst game of his All-American career. In a diary later published in *The Sporting News,* he wrote: "I couldn't concentrate all day during classes, mulling about what was going to happen. My head just wasn't in the game."

Clearly disoriented and confused by an uncertain future and anxiously awaiting the Navy's answer on his status, David took the floor in Halsey Field House on the evening of January 8th. For over two years, he had been as close to an unstoppable force as Navy basketball had ever manufactured. He had scored in double figures for a remarkable seventy-eight straight games and had led Navy to a twenty-one-game home winning streak. But he was not a machine.

Contributing to David's uncertain state of mind was Richmond Coach Dick Tarrant, who devised a unique defense to stop David, a variation on the standard diamond and one formation that often brought triple coverage on him inside. While the Spiders' two biggest men, 6-8 Steve Kratzer and 6-5, 235-pound Pete Woolfolk, sandwiched him between them, 6-4 Scott Stapleton joined them in Mr. Robinson's neighborhood, waving his arms in front of the Middies' center in an effort to deny him the ball.

It was unbelievably frustrating. The combination of his own state of mind and Richmond's aggressiveness took him out of his offensive game completely. On defense, his reactions were slow, and he kept picking up fouls for attempting blocks after being beaten by his man. He was called for his third personal with almost seven minutes left in the first half, and was forced to sit out until intermission. He started the second half, but picked up another foul less than five minutes later, and went right back to the bench. Once he reentered the game—almost ten minutes later—he hardly touched the ball, and when he did, he couldn't get a good shot.

The Spiders scored the last 13 points of the game to win 64-62. Since his sophomore year, David had never been so completely out of the flow. His performance was reflected in his line: 4-9 from the floor, 0-6 from the foul line, 9 rebounds, 6 blocks, and 5 fouls in just twenty-four minutes.

If he felt bad before the contest, he was utterly dejected after it. "I wasn't in the same gym tonight," he whispered, crushing an aluminum soda can in his hands. "I didn't move, didn't shoot well. I spent so much time on the bench, and then came back cold." Facing the press, David was at a loss for words. Finally, his father rescued him from the spotlight, put-

ting his arm around his son and leading him out of
the gym.

David's teammates were also shocked and dis-
mayed. His friend, Carl Liebert, said, "We really
needed him in the clutch. When he came back into
the game, we felt safe. And then he nearly shoots an
air ball. I hope David wakes up and realizes that if he
doesn't play, we aren't worth a damn."

On January 9th, retiring Secretary of the Navy
John H. Lehman released a statement: "Midshipman
David Robinson, at seven-foot-one, has been certified
as not physically qualified for a commission as an
unrestricted line officer in the U.S. Navy." He further
announced that David would be required to serve
two years of "restricted" duty, followed by four years
in the reserves.

David was told of the decision before the team
boarded a bus for Harrisonburg, Virginia, and a game
against James Madison. By the time the squad got off
the bus, his head was back in the game and he was
ready to play. With an awesome display of firepower,
Midshipman Robinson blew the Dukes out of their
own building. Navy won 95-70, and David was simply unstoppable, finishing with a school record 45
points and dominating the boards with 21 rebounds.

Later, David acknowledged what virtually everyone already knew, that his off-the-court worries had
gotten the best of him. "Two years is better than five
years," he commented. "I'm glad it's over and I know
what my future is going to be. I've probably been
more ruffled in the last three days than I've ever
been."

He was relieved, but that didn't necessarily make

his task of leading the Middies back to the NCAA
tournament a piece of cake. Opposing coaches, recognizing Navy's lack of offensive firepower outside
the center slot, invariably used collapsing zones on
Robinson. After his 45-point performance against
Madison, the Middies played George Mason. It was
no picnic; every time David touched the ball, three
men collapsed around him, pushing and bumping
him. He was held to a mere 10 shots and 21 points,
but the Middies still came away with the victory.

On January 25th, David took his game one notch
higher. For thirty-nine minutes and forty-six seconds,
he was inspired, a one-man fleet. But the game wasn't
against another CAA foe, it was against Kentucky in
Lexington's Rupp Arena. Finally, with fourteen seconds left, after it was clear that the outmanned Middies had no hope, Pete Herrmann gave up the ship
and pulled his aircraft carrier out of the contest. Suddenly more than 23,000 Kentucky partisans—and for
those who know college basketball, there's nobody
more partisan than a Wildcat fan—rose to their feet,
shouting and applauding for Midshipman David
Robinson. ABC's Dick Vitale also stood up at his
spot on press row—shouting even louder than usual.
And on the Kentucky bench, freshman phenom Rex
Chapman, whose long-distance bombing saved the
day for the Wildcats, stood and applauded, as did
Coach Eddie Sutton. Columnist Billy Reed of the
Lexington Herald-Leader was in hoops heaven. "No
disrespect intended," he wrote, "but Navy doesn't
have another player who could win a seat on the UK
bench." He said David's performance "may well
have been the best all-around game that anybody has

ever played against UK in the Wildcats' long and
shining history." Ramming home rim-rattling dunks,
shooting soft jumpers, racing downcourt on the wing
of the Navy fast break, and jumping out and swatting
away the shots of anyone who dared challenge him
inside, he hit 17-22 from the floor, 11-12 from the
line. He put together a triple-double, a remarkable
45-point, 14-rebound, 10-block masterpiece, against
one of college basketball's greatest traditions. "I've
seen every game David has played at the Academy,"
Pete Herrmann said, "and I think that was his best
overall."

David's peak performances were taking him beyond the status of a mere mortal and turning him into
a legend. Following the Kentucky game his buzzer-
beating 17-foot turnaround jumper enabled the Middies to squeak by with a 67-66 victory over North
Carolina-Wilmington. A few days later Navy came up
against an inspired James Madison team, intent on
revenge. Playing before a home crowd at Halsey, the
Middies just couldn't put the Dukes away. After
Madison hit a shot to give them a 71-70 lead with
just two seconds left, it looked like Madison was certain to pull off a big upset. Navy called time-out. The
Middies would have to take the ball out under their
own basket. There was only time, Coach Herrmann
reminded his players, for an inbounds pass and an
immediate shot. The coach told Doug Wojcik to take
the ball out, and ordered David to lose his man just
beyond midcourt, where Doug would hit him with
the pass. Before leaving the huddle, Herrmann reminded David not to put the ball on the floor, and to
shoot the ball, not just throw it up. The play worked

perfectly: Doug hit David with the pass, who turned toward the hoop and hit an amazing 40-foot bank shot to win the game 73-71. Halsey went wild, with waves of midshipmen rushing onto the court to carry off their hero.

Finally, it was February 21st, time for the Army-Navy showdown. The big game was even bigger than usual; it was the last home game of David's Navy career. This time there was less anticipation, less joy on the faces of the midshipmen as they saluted Tecumseh and asked for his help in overcoming the Cadets. Navy's greatest basketball era was about to come to an end. After four years, it was hard for David to believe it was almost over, but as the pregame ceremonies honored the graduating seniors, the reality began to sink in—this was it, he'd never play in Halsey again. David looked at his teammates with whom he'd shared so many good times, and he saw that at least two tough Middies—Doug Wojcik and Carl Liebert—were crying. He looked up in the stands and saw the tears in his mother's eyes too. All the pregame emotion seemed to drain the team of its spirit; when the game began, they came out flat. Meanwhile, Army's star guard Kevin Houston was lighting it up, bombing from the outside and scoring 27 points in the first half.

For four years David, Doug, Carl and their teammates had played one hard-fought game after another against the Cadets. The Middies didn't want it to end this way, with a loss to Army at home.

In the locker room at halftime, Coach Herrmann instructed Cliff Rees to tighten up his defense on Houston. With Army's sharpshooter effectively silenced after the intermission, and Navy's tall ship sweeping the boards, the Middies came back to win 58-52.

□

The postseason Colonial tournament looked like easy pickings for the Midshipmen, who finished their regular season conference schedule with a record of 13-1 (their only loss coming to Richmond in David's single digit horror show at Halsey). But after breezing past William & Mary and James Madison, Navy was taken to the limit by UNC-Wilmington in the championship game. It was a slow-paced defensive battle, pitting the two best centers in the league (David and the Seahawks' Brian Rowsom) against each other. With the rest of the Middies shooting a dismal 11 for 30, the offensive load fell squarely on David's shoulders. In the end, his 23 points were just enough to give Navy a 53-50 victory.

At the conference awards ceremony, David was honored as Conference Player of the Year and Tournament Most Valuable Player. Dick Vitale, the guest speaker, made repeated references to "The Admiral," his nickname for David. "Every time he mentioned me during the speech," wrote David in his diary, "my teammates would poke me and it was kind of embarrassing."

□

With the NCAA tournament coming up, it was clear to almost everyone that the Middies were not the squad that beat Syracuse and went to the Final Eight in '86. They were a one-dimensional team that would go only as far as their tall ship could carry them. But with David Robinson on board, they still had high hopes.

It was the first year of the three-pointer in college hoops' championship event, and Navy was matched up against Michigan, which had one of the best outside shooters in the country in Garde Thompson. It was clear from the start that Wolverine coach Bill Frieder would not challenge Robinson in the paint, but would instead try to spring Thompson and his other perimeter shooters for treys in order to force Navy out of its zone.

At first it was Navy's game. With David leading the charge by scoring 8 points in the first four minutes, the Middies surged into a 14-4 lead, and they still led by 10 with 10:41 remaining in the half. Then Thompson found the range, and even the premier shot-blocker in the nation couldn't stop him from hitting his treys.

Despite David's continuing domination of the paint, Navy began to unravel. By halftime, the Navy center had over half the Midshipman points, but the score was 49-44 Michigan, and Thompson had 20 points of his own on 6 of 8 from outside the 3-point line.

Navy struggled to stay close in the second half, but Michigan answered every one of David's dunks and short jumpers, often with a trey. With 5:42 to play, the score was 84-68 and the Middies' cause seemed lost. But they wouldn't give up. With David leading the charge, they stormed back, finally cutting the margin to 86-80 when David missed a 12-foot jumper, slid past the Michigan frontline, and jammed home the rebound with 2:42 left for his twenty-first basket of the game. It was a spectacular play, but it was Navy's last gasp.

The Middies slowly expired. Their center, who had carried the team on his shoulders all year, could carry them no farther. David Robinson's college career was coming to an end.

With two seconds left and the game impossible to salvage, Michigan's Loy Vaught went in for a slam dunk. His spectacular play ended with him back on the ground, and the rim sitting at a 45-degree angle. With the clock stopped and the rim being repaired, Pete Herrmann had the chance to take David out. Navy's all-time leader in thirty-three statistical categories was leaving a Navy game for the last time. He had led the Middies to the national rankings for the first time ever, and in his four years at the Academy helped his school compile a brilliant 106-25 record. David was the first player in NCAA history to score 2,500 points (he finished with 2,619), grab 1,300 rebounds (he got 1,306) and hit 60 percent of his shots from the floor. He was also the first Middie ever selected as a first team All-American. And he was honored that very day with the Naismith Award, as college basketball's Player of the Year.

By the time he stepped off the floor in Charlotte, North Carolina, on March 12, 1987, he had scored 50 points. His performance that night, capping his remarkable college career, was one of the greatest in NCAA tournament history. It was the highest point total ever for a Midshipman. And when he took his seat, the cheering continued unabated for several minutes.

When the applause finally died down, David put his hand over his heart and joined his fellow Middies in singing "Navy Blue and Gold." He then told his teammates. "No matter where I go or what I do the rest of my life, I'll never forget you guys. If you ever need anything, don't be afraid to come to me and ask for help."

Strangers came up to congratulate him, to seek his autograph, to make contact with the twenty-one-year-old Midshipman who had rewritten the Navy—and NCAA—record books. He was being touted as the next Bill Russell, the next Kareem, one of the greatest big men ever. He enjoyed the glory, but recognized that some values were more important than riches and fame. Later David reflected on the meaning of his four years in Annapolis.

"The lights are out, the hype is over and the cheers have subsided," he said. "Those things come and go. It's the friendships with my teammates that I'll cherish forever. They are the kinds of things that I'll carry with me the rest of my life."

□

The season was over, but the honors kept pouring in. Suddenly David was a full-blown celebrity, the amazing Middie, the soft-spoken superman, the clean-cut American role model to end all role models. And everyone wanted a piece of him.

As soon as Navy was eliminated from the 1987 NCAA tournament, the image of the tall, intelligent, young black man was literally everywhere. David charmed Jane Pauley on the *Today* show, hung out at New York's Hard Rock Cafe with the rock group

Chicago and other show biz types (some of whom asked *him* for his autograph), and logged over 16,000 miles of air travel in three weeks. He patiently cooperated with over fifty major interviewers, and smilingly received a seemingly endless array of awards. On the surface, he remained the same unspoiled, modest young man he had always been. When asked about all the attention, he simply shrugged and said, "I guess it goes with the territory."

The last week of March was a nonstop run of appearances, awards, and commitments, a far cry from the day less than four years earlier that he took his first plane ride, stayed in his first hotel, and was given the nickname "Country" by his teammates.

David's home base of Annapolis seemed, during those hectic weeks, to be little more than a way station on his way to somewhere else. He returned home on Tuesday, and less than a day later was off for Kentucky, where he joined the Bluegrass State's Governor Martha Lane Collins in a "Champions Against Drugs" program. On Thursday he flew from Lexington to New Orleans, where he would watch the Final Four, star in an all-star game, and receive the Rupp Award as player of the year, having outpolled his closest rival—Indiana's Steve Alford—by a record margin.

On Monday, April 1st, David continued on to Los Angeles, where an assembly of 1,000 sportswriters, editors, and broadcasters named him the winner of the nation's most prestigious player of the year honor—the John R. Wooden Award—also by the largest margin in history.

On Thursday David was in Atlanta to receive the Naismith Player of the Year Award and be praised by Indiana, and former Army, Coach "General" Bob Knight.

For most of the next year, the trophies and awards kept piling in. Not only was he everyone's player of year, but he also received the NCAA's Top Six Award (the organization's highest honor), was named the nation's outstanding men's amateur athlete by the U.S. Sports Academy, and was a finalist for the prestigious Sullivan Award, given each year to the top amateur athlete in the United States—male or female.

But first it was back to Annapolis on Friday for the Naval Academy's Basketball Awards dinner.

At the Navy dinner 300 guests heard Captain Doug Wojcik, his voice breaking with emotion, talk about the last three years of Middie hoops. It began with "Division III Gettysburg," he recalled. "Who would have dreamed what was to come between Gettysburg three years ago and Michigan of the Big Ten, the team that ended those three years."

After Superintendent Ronald F. Marryott of the Naval Academy announced that Navy was officially retiring the number 50, Midshipman David Robinson took the podium and said, "It's so hard to go to awards banquets all across the country and explain about the bond we all have between us. To hear the things Doug Wojcik and other friends said about me tonight makes me feel better than anything.

"It's nice to pick up all these awards, but it's more important what your friends and the people you care about think and say about you.

"It thrills me to be able to say thanks to the people here, people who have supported our team all year. I want to tell you my life has been a dream walk."

He thanked his parents, the loyal Navy fans, "but most of all I want to thank my teammates. Without them I wouldn't be what I am today."

On Monday David was back on a plane—off to Honolulu to play in the Aloha Classic.

Of course the celebrity had its effects on him. His adeptness at juggling time was stretched beyond even his limits; his schoolwork suffered, and some of his other earlier priorities fell by the wayside.

He was also learning to become more protective of his privacy and his time alone. He had never been able to just fade into the background, but now he was no longer just another tall black man. He was David Robinson and he could never again be anonymous.

Although he was still formally a student at the Naval Academy, David was beginning to look away from it, to assess its impact upon him from a new, more distant perspective. "I don't regret coming," he said. "This was the best place for me my first two years. Hindsight is always the best sight. If I'd known I was going to grow to be 7-1, of course I would have gone somewhere else. If I'd known that my basketball was going to develop like it did, of course I would have gone somewhere else."

Soon, he knew, he would leave the Academy behind him.

□

The United States Naval Academy class of 1987 consisted of 1,022 graduates (76 percent of those who had entered as plebes four years earlier). Among them were 57 Hispanic-Americans, 37 Asian-Americans, 36 African-Americans, 3 Native-Americans, and 70 women. There were 105 math majors and more than two dozen All-American athletes.

The graduates' joy at completing the Academy's rigorous program, and their anticipation about becoming commissioned officers, was tempered by shock and dismay at the previous week's unprovoked Iraqi missile attack on the U.S.S. *Stark,* which caused the deaths of thirty-seven American sailors.

The traditional commencement exercise of scaling the 21-foot-high Herndon monument in front of the chapel took the longest time ever—more than three hours.

Speakers included Vice President George Bush and Secretary of the Navy James Webb.

It was not an event for the impatient.

The commencement itself took place in Halsey Field House, the site of some of the Class of '87's fondest memories. One by one, each of the thirty-six companies of midshipmen approached the podium, where they were to receive their diplomas from the Vice President.

The *Baltimore Evening Sun* reported that when the 20th company was moving toward the stage, a professor emeritus walked over and asked one tall young graduate for his autograph; he obliged, then looked at the middie in front of him, rolled his eyes, and shrugged. It comes with the territory, he seemed to be saying.

Finally, after the last member of the 36th company got his diploma, the graduates shouted "Beat Army!" and threw their hats in the air.

Soon thereafter, the *Annapolis Capital,* citing the record of the Class of '87's most prominent graduate both on and off the court, editorialized, "Children will look to David Robinson as a role model on the basketball court. May they also remember him as a scholar and gentleman."

CHAPTER VIII

MIXED MESSAGES

During the fall of 1986, Ensign Napoleon McCallum carried two tough full-time jobs—one as a Naval officer and the other as a running back for the Los Angeles Raiders—while Midshipman First Class David Robinson, 20th Company, watched with a great deal of interest. If Nap showed that he could both play pro ball and serve in the officers' corps, the Navy had no reason to deny their star center the opportunity of playing in the NBA the year after he graduated from the Academy.

Nap came through with flying colors, and on December 22nd, Secretary of the Navy John H. Lehman gave an unequivocal answer to the *Navy Times* and to David on the question of moonlighting: "To me," he said, "every and any officer and enlisted man will have the McCallum rule apply; they can go and do in their own time things that do not conflict with their obligations."

The Secretary dismissed all the objections that had been raised regarding his ruling on McCallum, saying, "I'm totally confident and comfortable that it was the right decision. There's no doubt that it's been in the best interest of the Navy. He wants to stay Navy and tells everybody he does. It gives us a chance to flash to so many American families the standards of quality that are run-of-the-mill in the Navy.''

Two weeks later, when Secretary Lehman announced his finding on Midshipman David Robinson's status, declaring that the Middies' star basketball player was "not physically qualified for a commission as an unrestricted line officer" and that he would be assigned to serve two years of "restricted" duty and four years in the reserves, it was with the clear understanding that Midshipman Robinson could do exactly what Ensign McCallum was doing—play pro ball while serving on active duty, as long as it didn't conflict with his U.S. Navy obligations.

Although David was disappointed that he would have to serve, he was relieved that the Navy had stuck by its guns and kept the promises they'd made to him back in his sophomore year. Now, it seemed, if he wanted to play in the NBA next season, there was very little standing in his way.

□

Nobody—not Secretary Lehman, not the Naval Academy brass, nor David himself—could have foreseen the firestorm of controversy that the Secretary's decisions engendered.

Letter writers in newspapers across the country declared their positions—should Robinson play or serve, and could he play and serve at the same time?

On February 25th, at a Congressional hearing on

the Defense Department manpower budget request, the new chairman of the House Armed Services Subcommittee on Military Personnel and Compensation, Maryland Democrat Beverly Byron, declared that the decisions on McCallum and Robinson "send the wrong signal to many other military personnel who are unable to get special privileges."

By late winter, the perception had overtaken the reality. Early in March, Chapman B. Cox, speaking for the Department of Defense, said the Pentagon is "very concerned about the image or perception of special treatment" for athletes. "We have been assured there is no special treatment and when Ensign McCallum gets orders he will move under orders."

Later that month, soon after David's brilliant college basketball finale, it was announced that Secretary Lehman would be leaving his post and that President Reagan had selected James H. Webb, a best-selling author, Vietnam veteran, and graduate of the Naval Academy, as his successor. Secretary-designate Webb immediately made his opposition to his predecessor's "arrangement" with officer-athletes crystal clear.

David, who was right in the middle of his Player of the Year victory tour, responded to the changing atmosphere in the press. When asked whether Webb would honor the Navy's previous decision, David replied, "I have an agreement with the Navy, and anything else that's been said is just speculative. So I really shouldn't comment on that."

In the middle of the Final Four, David told the assembled media: "They made a contract with me and we have a commitment. I don't know if he can

rescind it or not. I don't think he can." When asked
why the new Secretary had to maintain the status quo
ante, David replied, "It's a rule of office that someone cannot rescind a policy that the predecessor
made. I think that's the case, but I'm not sure."

In a vain attempt to tip the balance of public
pressure in his favor, he called the Secretary-designate "obviously opinionated." Yet even though he
seemed to be wearing his feelings on his sleeve, his
criticism stopped far short of insubordination. "I'm a
member of the United States Navy," he said, "and
like anybody else I'm subject to what he decides if he
is confirmed."

Two days later, outgoing Navy Secretary Lehman
declared that he still felt he had made the proper
ruling on officers moonlighting as athletes. He said
both David and Nap were excellent role models and
that minority applications had "skyrocketed" since
they became public figures. He also pointed out that
David "generated more than nine hundred thousand
dollars for the Academy by getting the team to the
NCAA tournament," an amount that far offset the
cost of his Navy education.

Although the Navy is an institution with many
hundreds of thousands of employees, a multibillion-
dollar budget, and a primary responsibility of defending the interests and security of the United States, it
seemed as though the major issue confronting James
Webb in his Senate confirmation hearings as Navy
chief executive was the status of two young athletes.
There were clearly differences of opinion among the
Senators, with neither Democrats nor Republicans in
agreement about the correct course of action. Com-

mittee chairman Sam Nunn of Georgia and William
Cohen of Maine were both noncommittal. But the
Robinson family's own Senator, former Navy Secretary John Warner of Virginia, supported retiring Secretary Lehman's position and declared that "the Secretary of the Navy must be given maximum flexibility
to make judgments." Senator John Chafee of Rhode
Island was vehement in his opposition, declaring, "It
would be a mistake for the Navy to play favorites. He
[David] should fulfill his commitment. He knew the
commitment when he accepted the appointment and
he's been given a free education, in fact been paid for
being in the Navy." And the nominee himself, testify-
ing before the full Senate Armed Services Committee, said, "I believe that the taxpayers who contribute
$130,000 [the approximate value of a Midshipman's
education] deserve the full value for their money."

On April 3rd, the *Annapolis Capital* urged incoming secretary Webb to honor the Navy's commitments to Midshipman Robinson. "The Navy places
great value on honor," the editorial read. "Nothing is
more honorable than a man—and the institution he
leads—keeping a promise. If the Navy expects its future officers to respect the code of honor, it must
keep its word to David Robinson."

On April 6th, although Captain Pat Donnelly of
the Naval Academy was still declaring that "The
Navy will wait until David's drafted and see if there's
a billet in that city before making any decisions on
where to assign him," the wind appeared to be shift-
ing. The NBA, of course, was willing to do anything
to accommodate the Navy's needs, as long as they
could get the All-American ensign, even on a part-

time basis. New York Knick scout Dick McGuire, en-
visioning Robinson and Patrick Ewing playing side by
side as a minifleet of aircraft carriers, commented,
"We'd build a Naval station on top of Madison
Square Garden if we could get him." But James
Webb, sailing through his confirmation hearings, was
unyielding.

While David was meeting with the top athletes'
agents in the country, trying to make a decision on
who would represent him in his dealings with the
NBA, his chances of playing pro ball the following
fall were disappearing.

On the second Friday in April, James H. Webb
was sworn in as the sixty-sixth Secretary of the Navy.
The following Tuesday, after a Navy spokesman acknowledged that Midshipman David Robinson and
his family met with "senior Naval officials at the
Academy" during his sophomore year who assured
him he would not be bound to serve five years upon
graduation, the secretary made his first major decision in office.

In a lengthy prepared statement, Webb granted
an exception to Robinson, declaring "It is clear to me
from a full review of the facts that Midshipman
Robinson understood that some accommodation
would be made concerning his service obligation that
would permit him to play professional basketball
during at least a portion of his period of obligated
service. . . .

"I believe that Midshipman Robinson relied in
good faith on that understanding in arriving at his
decision to remain at the Academy at a time when he
would not have been committed to active duty ser-

vice had he resigned. Consequently," he said, "it would now be unfair to require him to serve on active duty for five years."

Without assigning blame, Webb implied that although he would not have made the same agreement, he accepted it as binding. He would honor the Navy's previously stated commitment to Robinson and allow him to serve just two years of active duty instead of the usual five.

"That's good news for the seven lottery teams," declared an exultant San Antonio Spurs General Manager Bob Bass. "There is obviously nobody close to him. He's No. 1."

But while former Navy Secretary Lehman had allowed Napoleon McCallum to play football with the Los Angeles Raiders on a "not-to-interfere" basis while on active duty, Webb's statement reversed the policy, banning "any special preference with regard to choice of duty assignments or any other decision regarding . . . military responsibilities." Secretary Webb continued, "he will be treated the same as his peers," and reiterated his basic philosophy regarding moonlighting: "The military in general, and the duties of commissioned officers in particular, constitute a full-time profession."

David was the lucky one. Because he was 7-1, he would be commissioned as a "restricted line officer" with only two years of active duty; Napoleon McCallum would have to serve out his full five years before he could resume his professional football career.

The next day, David responded to Secretary Webb's statement by saying that he had not yet had a chance to review his options. "I don't know how much trouble it would be to play pro," he said. "But I haven't had a chance to sit down and look at everything. Basically, I'll do whatever's best for me."

Despite David's uncertainty, a Navy spokesman, Mark D. Neuhart, was quite clear about David's lack of choice. "Under the new policy announced by Secretary Webb, no, there is no way he could play professional basketball. He will continue to be permitted to participate in amateur athletics, including the Olympics."

USA Today analyzed David's situation and reported that he could sign an NBA contract, receive a signing bonus, and enter into endorsement contracts yet still remain an amateur. "He's not a professional until he lines up on the court or is entered in the scorebook of a regular-season game," said Bill Wall, executive director of ABA-USA, amateur basketball's governing body. "If he enters a trust fund, then he could endorse products and still retain amateur eligibility. Money would be funneled into a trust fund, and checks would be written for his living expenses."

The Secretary's statement unleashed a firestorm of controversy in the press, with the media serving up a mixed bag of opinions and solutions. One of the more intriguing suggestions, in *The Sporting News*, called for five years of Naval service to be served *during the off-season only*. The commitment could be served over the course of ten years, but it would be served. And the officer-athlete could have his cake and eat it too.

A *Washington Post* editorial, entitled "Duty First," praised the reversal of policy, declaring that "it reemphasizes the primacy of duty, telling all those now serving that what they do is important. For another, it will help keep sports in their place at Annapolis—as something that has to be worked into a demanding schedule of training, study, and other activities aimed at producing good officers."

Post columnist Thomas Boswell had an entirely different point of view, calling the Secretary's action "ill-advised" and comparing it, as his first act in office, to "stepping on deck and falling overboard." Boswell said, "McCallum had to imitate the Labors of Hercules to do an honest job as ensign and still be a Raiders standout. Tales of his round-the-clock perseverance—all because he wanted to fulfill his Navy dream so badly that he refused to leave Annapolis after his sophomore year to attend a football factory —must have made many teen-agers think, perhaps for the first time, that a Navy officer's life might be as worthwhile as a glamorous NFL career. You can't buy that kind of gut-level recruiting. Not in the general population. And especially not among blacks, who long have been justifiably tepid toward careers as commissioned military officers.

"By considering McCallum's special skills and abilities to help the Navy, Lehman was showing that, after you paid your dues and proved you could cut the mustard, the brass would treat you like a peacetime individual and not a wartime pawn."

Boswell wrote of Webb: "Seems the new boss wants to show who's boss." He said both McCallum and Robinson deserved better treatment than they were getting, and that "Throughout their Navy years . . . at junctures where they could have left the Academy at little or no cost, McCallum and Robinson

asked for signs from on high. They took the risk of
accepting the unseen brass at its word, or rather at its
wink. Play ball, be an A-plus midshipman and we'll
treat you fairly. That was the unspoken, unwritten
quid pro quo. Navy took the recruiting benefits, the
football gate receipts and pocketed the $900,000 in
NCAA tournament money that was a direct result of
Robinson's play. In return, the Navy bent rules for
McCallum and Robinson but never broke one or
made a new one. The jocks asked no public favors
and saluted every step of the way.

"In light of this, what Webb intends to do
amounts to welching."

John Feinstein, also writing for *The Washington
Post,* stated, "As long as Robinson waits those 18
months [until after the Olympics], the Navy gets its
all-American symbol. Robinson gets to be a hero
first, a millionaire shortly thereafter. It isn't a bad
deal—for anyone."

The controversy raged in the *Annapolis Capital*
too. Sports editor Al Hopkins applauded Secretary
Webb's decision, saying "The Academy does not exist
to train professional athletes or Naval Academy re-
cruiters. Its sole purpose is to train naval officers."
But the *Capital*'s editorial disagreed: "The Navy obviously feels that changing the rules in the middle of
the game is all right. What it really boils down to is
the fact that the secretary of the Navy plays 'God'
and what he says goes—no questions, please.

"When you are playing with the lives of young
men," the *Capital* writer continued, "this should not
be the way things are run."

Writing in the *Baltimore Sun,* Mike Littwin

David takes an alley oop from a teammate for a slam dunk over Cleveland State in his Navy days.

David captures a
loose ball in a
Navy game.

Navy coach Pete
Herrmann con-
gratulates David
near the end of
their game against
Michigan after
David was named
winner of the
annual Naismith
Award.

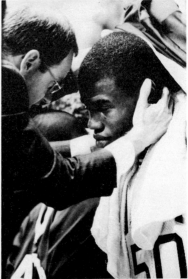

Then–Vice President George Bush chats with David during a 1987 visit to the White House.

Legendary retired UCLA coach John Wooden congratulates David at the 1987 Wooden Award ceremonies, where the Navy senior won the award as the top collegiate basketball player in the nation.

At the 1987 Naval Academy graduation exercises
David stands with—and above—fellow midshipmen.

CRAIG STAFFORD

David's mother, Frieda (seated), pores over the young superstar's fan mail.

David clowns around with his brother Chuck.

AP/WIDE WORLD PHOTOS

David and Spurs teammate Terry Cummings in the recording studio.

David at the diving-control station aboard the sub USS *Buffalo*.

David drives the
baseline against
the Houston
Rockets' Akeem
Olajuwon.

David goes up
against the New
York Knicks'
Patrick Ewing.

called the two Navy athletes "good citizens both, good students both, ambassadors, if you will, for the Navy way in a time when a lot of good men are needed." After asserting that both had already more than paid their way through the Academy, he concluded, "If Robinson had decided to transfer, you can bet that any Secretary of the Navy, Webb included, would have spent any part of the necessary 24 hours it takes to be an officer attempting to persuade Robinson to stay."

All the jawboning in the world didn't change the facts—it was a done deal. Nap McCallum could, in all likelihood, kiss his football career good-bye, and David Robinson would have to make do, for the time being, with taking the NBA's money, but playing only for his country.

While the NBA conducted its draft, David was in the White House brunching with Vice President Bush. He was sure to be the day's top pick, but he was in no hurry to sign a pro contract. For the next two years, he already had a job.

Ensign David Robinson was ordered to report for duty on July 1st, 1987, at the Navy's submarine base at King's Bay, Georgia.

CHAPTER IX

SAN ANTONIO'S
$26 MILLION MAN

It was the last chance saloon for the San Antonio Spurs. For the Alamo city, which knew all about lost causes, it appeared inevitable after the 1986–87 campaign that they would soon be left high and dry without an NBA franchise.

The Spurs had won only twenty-eight games that season, making it their worst year on the court in team history. And they weren't doing any better at the gate. They'd placed twenty-second out of twenty-three teams in the league in attendance, drawing barely 8,000 people a game for their eighth consecutive annual decline.

Team owner Angelo Drossos, known for his "frugality," openly declared, "If the Spurs continue not to draw, and by continue I am talking about next year, [moving the franchise] is something we will have to look at."

And although Drossos's cost-cutting measures (particularly with the team payroll) had actually enabled him to turn a half-million dollar profit in '86–'87, despite the disastrous attendance and low TV revenue, he stated unequivocally, "I'm not in the philanthropic business."

If the Spurs didn't win the NBA draft lottery—and with it rights to Midshipman David Robinson—on May 17th, it was clear to just about everyone that they were history as far as San Antonio was concerned.

Willing to go to any lengths to maintain interest in their hapless hoopsters, Spurs' management held a "lucky charm" contest among their dwindling faithful, hoping to find a talisman that would influence the stars and get them the first choice in the lottery. Faced with such a disastrous civic scenario, the citizens of the river city turned out in force in an attempt to ensure the survival of the team. On the last day of the contest, Postal Service safety expert Roberto Pachecano outdid the standard rabbit's feet and four leaf clovers with his Texas style bolo tie, replete with red chameleon. "Lore has it," explained Pachecano, a former Marine and son of a sailor, "that if shipwrecked sailors found a red chameleon, they would survive." (And, he might have added, if the fortunate seafarers managed to find their way home, they would be granted—heaven help us—early discharges from the Navy.)

With the help of Roberto Pachecano's red reptile, the Spurs won the lottery—and the right to select the draft's biggest prize since Patrick Ewing went to the New York Knicks in 1985.

Despite their mediocrity on the court, the Spurs already had some fine young players, starting with

All-Star guard Alvin Robertson and rookie Johnny Dawkins. If they could get David Robinson, along with other lottery picks in the next two years, they were in a position to build a contender.

David was a franchise player, and the Spurs' management was willing to wait as long as they had to for their tall ship to come in. "It's like when we put a one million dollar contract in the lap of Robert Parish's mother when we were trying to sign him after his junior year," Drossos told the *Baltimore Evening Sun.* "She said, 'No, I don't want him to play pro ball. I want him to finish school. We've been poor this long, one more year won't make any difference.' " Or in this case, two more.

Drossos saw David as the Spurs' savior. Robinson, he declared, "can almost walk on water. He can certainly walk on the San Antonio River." And because of his team's previous penurious salary structure, Drossos was willing—and able—to stake the ranch on signing him.

Early speculation was that Robinson would command at least one million dollars a year in salary. But on draft day, despite winning the lottery, there was no assurance that the Spurs could actually *get* David for any amount of money.

With his two-year military service commitment, David was in a unique position. According to the NBA's own rules, he could simply not sign a contract for a year and be eligible to go back into the draft. If he was still dissatisfied with the team that won the rights to him, he could wait another year—and become an unrestricted free agent, just as he was being discharged from the Navy.

Rick Barry, working as an analyst on superstation WTBS, predicted that the Spurs would not be able to sign Robinson, and said that it would be in his best interests to wait until San Antonio's rights to him expired, and then sign with the team of his choice.

"It's a simple supply and demand," explained Barry succinctly. "There's one outstanding basketball player and he will be in demand by twenty-three teams. . . . You'll probably never have an athlete in this position again. Why shouldn't he take advantage of it?"

By the time of the draft, David had already publicized his wish list. Playing alongside Magic as Abdul-Jabbar's successor in Los Angeles, he said, "looks good to me," as did joining the Celtics in the waning years of Robert Parish's career. He was also intrigued by the idea of teaming with Michael Jordan in Chicago and indicated that he would definitely consider staying home in D.C. with the Washington Bullets. He would even go to Cleveland, where he had some good friends among the younger Cavs players. But San Antonio? That was another story.

Spurs' General Manager Bob Bass spoke to David several times before the June 22nd NBA draft. On June 3rd, he was quoted in *The San Antonio Sun* as saying, "We want David to come down here, see our arena and the city, meet the coaches and the team, and learn something about our franchise." The ensign, on his part, was noncommittal, but he was "trying to keep an open mind about it."

If friendly persuasion didn't work, the Spurs knew there were other ways of trying to convince

David to relocate to South Texas. And the league, fearing a threat to the linchpin of its system—the player draft—was more than willing to back them.

Less than a week after San Antonio's lottery victory, there was already speculation that the Spurs would invoke a little-used bylaw in the NBA constitution, known as the "Armed Services Rule," in order to retain the rights to David and prevent him from signing with another team. The rule, originally put into effect thirty-seven years earlier *to protect the rights of players* whose careers were interrupted by military service, would be given a new interpretation. While the bylaw had once insured that armed forces draftees would not be cut by their teams while serving in the military, it would now, according to the league's interpretation, allow the Spurs to retain exclusive rights to Ensign Robinson until a month after his military obligation ended.

The league was fully committed to the Spurs. They knew that if Robinson was allowed to walk away from the draft and sign with the team of his choice, he would be throwing a monkey wrench into the whole draft procedure. Commissioner David Stern said he'd like to see the Spurs sign David, and league officials made their support of the team's legal position a matter of principle.

On the other side of the ledger, advocates for the players, like CBS Announcer and NBA Hall of Famer Tom Heinsohn, wanted David to fight the Armed Services Rule. Heinsohn said that invoking the bylaw "would be taking Robinson's options away under the collective bargaining agreement," and warned that if the league chose to proceed with their course of action, "Robinson might bring down the whole draft structure."

Of course a protracted legal battle would be in nobody's interest.

If David was unwilling to sign with the Spurs at any price, many observers thought it was more likely that the team would trade its rights to him for a combination of players and draft picks. In the days surrounding the draft, beat writers throughout America speculated on possible packages: Bob Ryan of *The Boston Globe* suggested Robinson for Kevin McHale, Reggie Lewis, and a No. 1 draft pick; Gordon Edes of the *Los Angeles Times* thought the Lakers might offer James Worthy, Byron Scott, and a No. 1; *Newsday*'s Gerry Sullivan's scenario had the Knicks parting with Patrick Ewing and Rory Sparrow for a shot at David. Other predictions had Milwaukee offering Terry Cummings and Paul Pressey and Cleveland giving the Spurs Brad Daugherty and Ron Harper. Wherever he might go, Robinson's value—two full years before he expected to put on an NBA uniform—was extraordinarily high. But in July, before talks even began with the recalcitrant Robinson, Angelo Drossos insisted he would say no to all the proposed deals. "There isn't any trade that we would make for David Robinson," he told the *San Antonio Light*. "A year from now, a month from now, or a week from now, maybe I'll feel differently. But right now, if Chicago was to call me and say, 'we'll give you Michael Jordan,' I would not make the trade. Or Houston, if they said, 'we would give you Olajuwon,' we would not make the trade either."

The Spurs were fully committed to bringing David Robinson to San Antonio.

□

But before San Antonio could negotiate with David, first they had to have someone to negotiate with. And the competition among agents for the right to represent the ensign was as public, and as hard-fought, as any game David ever played in his college career.

The Player of the Year would clearly be represented by one of pro sports' top agents, someone who was capable of maximizing his potential earnings both on and off the court. But it also had to be someone who was willing to go along with the military situation; he and his family did not want anyone who might make waves publicly, thereby tarnishing David's solid-gold, All-American image.

By early June, when Bob Bass tried to reach David on the phone and was told he'd gone on a four-day fishing trip with his father, the ensign was very close to making a decision. Speculation on the finalists centered on Boston-based Bob Woolf and two Washington, D.C. agencies, ProServ and Advantage International. Still in the running but considered more of a long shot was Larry Fleischer, who was also the executive director of the NBA Players Association.

The finalists had pulled out all the stops in wooing Ensign Robinson. As far back as April, ProServ agent David Falk had been seen talking with David and his brother Chuck at a Bullets game. Another ProServ agent, Donald Dell, had arranged for him to meet the agency's reigning superstar, Michael Jordan, who talked with David about how it feels to score 50 points in a game and lose. Michael went out of his way to include Chuck in the conversation, which ranged from cars to sea stories. And he also gave the older Robinson brother some idea of the advantages of being a ProServ client.

In June, Boston attorney/agent Bob Woolf, whose client list included Larry Bird, flew David and UNLV's Armon Gilliam from Las Vegas (where they had attended a college awards ceremony) to Los Angeles, where they were met by a limo which whisked them directly to game three of the NBA finals. (The Forum crowd, with visions of Magic and David leading the Lakers back to the championship, chanted "Wait two years," but Robinson maintained his open mind about the Spurs.) After the Los Angeles sighting, it was assumed that Woolf had gained the inside track.

The third contender, Lee Fentress of Advantage International, was a Washington-based agent whose 150-plus clients included Hakeem Olajuwon, Brad Daugherty, Sam Perkins, Maurice Cheeks, Moses Malone, Danny Ainge, and numerous athletes in other sports. Over the years, Fentress had also represented several Spurs, including Larry Kenon, George Karl, and Jeff Cook. Fentress was known as a tough negotiator who got top dollar for his clients. He had negotiated often with Drossos, even played tennis with the Spurs' owner, and the two trusted each other to put all their cards on the table and not negotiate in the press and the forum of public opinion.

For the Spurs, the biggest concern was that David would report for duty without choosing an agent. If he didn't have representation, they knew there could be no substantive negotiations. And that meant they could run out of time and lose their rights to him without ever having the chance to make an offer.

Thus, when Lee Fentress of Advantage International was announced as David's agent just days before the draft, the Spurs' management team breathed a collective sigh of relief. "We're real happy about it," declared Bob Bass. And Angelo Drossos concurred wholeheartedly, praising Fentress as an agent who "understands when to close a deal."

□

When the Spurs formally named David Robinson the No. 1 pick in the 1987 NBA draft on June 22nd, they knew they were months away from coming to an agreement, because less than a week before David settled on Fentress, a league-wide moratorium on signing (or even negotiating) with rookies and free agents was announced. Both the owners and the players' association had agreed to the ban in the hope that it would speed the process of hammering out a new collective bargaining agreement. The two sides agreed that the prohibition would remain in force until either October 1st, or a new basic agreement was signed, whichever came first.

Players Association executive director Larry Fleischer told the Spurs they couldn't talk contract at all with Robinson, "the theory being you may not have any rights to him." And after negotiations for a new labor-management agreement broke down over the issue of the draft, nine players—including Armon

Gilliam, Rory Sparrow, Junior Bridgeman, Reggie Lewis, Darrell Walker, and David Robinson—filed an antitrust class-action suit against the NBA for restraint of trade. The litigation, which challenged the college draft, the salary cap, and the owners' right-of-first-refusal on free agents, was, in fact, a serious attempt by the players to force the owners to negotiate changes in the key issues in dispute. And despite the NBA's initial response, that they were "comfortable with [their] legal position," it eventually helped push the negotiations forward so that the league was able to avoid the bitterness of a strike or lockout, which had plagued both the NFL and Major League Baseball in recent years.

However, neither the ban on substantive negotiations nor the suit against the league prevented David and Lee Fentress from having contact with the Spurs. Money could be dealt with later, after the legal hurdles had been removed. For now, the most important question was where David wanted to live and work.

The fact which so many people found so hard to understand was that he really was open-minded. He had not already decided to hold out and accept a contract to play only in L.A. or Boston. He was ready to be convinced.

And the Spurs—along with the entire city of San Antonio—were ready for some friendly, Texas-style persuasion.

In a larger city, the municipal focus could never have been so clearly set upon a single objective as it was in San Antonio after the Spurs drafted David Robinson. One could never imagine Los Angeles, New York, Chicago, or even Dallas or Detroit turning the pursuit of a professional athlete into a civic mission. But because San Antonio is such a small market (the nation's forty-fifth largest in television) and metropolitan area, it became important psychologically for both the team and the town to overcome the perception that they were "too small" to compete with the L.A.s and New Yorks. In the end, the low-key intimacy of the south Texas city worked to the Spurs' advantage, enabling them to enlist the community support they needed to woo Mr. Robinson to their neighborhood.

Soon after the lottery, U.S. Rep. Albert Bustamente of San Antonio wrote Secretary of the Navy Webb asking that the ensign be stationed near the city and be allowed to play for the Spurs in the coming year.

Municipal leaders including Mayor Henry Cisneros also participated in the effort to bring David to the Alamo City.

The Spurs pulled out all the big guns in their arsenal, including the Naval Academy's own Heisman Trophy-winning quarterback and resident Texas legend, Roger Staubach. "My first choice would have been for him to be a Dallas Maverick," said Staubach, who publicly tried to convince his fellow middie to sign with a team from the Lone Star State, "but after that, the next best thing would have been for him to get to San Antonio or Houston."

At times it seemed as if the entire city was coming out to welcome the tall sailor.

David, meanwhile, wanted to be in a situation where he felt comfortable. In his public statements, he generally spoke about his desire to be with "a good organization," to "have a good relationship with the general managers and the owners," and to "be on a team with a good attitude . . . that's concerned about winning."

Ambrose Robinson, however, had a slightly different take on his son's priorities. "I think David will have to enjoy the environment in San Antonio or he won't want to play there," he reasoned. "I think that's more important than how stable the franchise is. He hasn't even heard much about the environment around San Antonio, except the Riverwalk and the Alamo, much less being able to experience them." And David said, "I want to see the attitude of the people."

In many ways, San Antonio offered an almost ideal situation for the high-powered prospect. If David had gone to the Lakers or Celtics, the pressure for immediate success would have been enormous; anything less than a league championship would have been considered a failure. The glare of the national media can be pitiless; it has been known to destroy athletes' confidence in their skills.

David had been able to develop as a college ballplayer in a low-profile program with no great expectations—he had come into the spotlight through the back door. He had thrived in the role of the underdog, the giant killer. It was a role he was familiar with. Now, despite his own advance billing as a "franchise" player, the pressure to win with the Spurs, who played thousands of miles from the national spotlight, was far less immediate than it would have been in Boston or L.A. In San Antonio, success could come in increments; to bring in the fans, it wasn't necessary to do much more than show improvement.

Soon after the draft, the Spurs asked David to visit their organization and their city and he accepted the invitation. On July 16th, in a phone interview with the *San Antonio Light*'s Jim Lefko from Lee Fentress's office, David asked that San Antonio not roll out the red carpet when he came. "That's not my style," he insisted. "I'm a lot more mellow."

Still, the city proceeded with its plans to welcome the young ensign. On September 15th, it was reported that David had received permission from his commanding officer at King's Bay Naval Base to travel to San Antonio for the weekend. Three days later at the crack of dawn, David's mother, father, brother Chuck, and cousin Aldrich Mitchell, along with Lee Fentress, boarded a chartered jet in Washington, D.C. After picking up David at King's Bay, they proceeded on to San Antonio, where they were met by Mayor Cisneros, 700 fans, a roomful of government officials, and a mariachi band. In the welcoming ceremony, David was given a significant promotion: Ensign David Maurice Robinson, U.S.N., became an honorary admiral in the Texas navy.

In the next two days, David was taken for a helicopter tour of the city with the mayor as his guide; he played golf and tennis at one of the city's most exclusive country clubs and was wined and dined at its top restaurants. He met with Spurs' officials and with some of the players. The city waited anxiously for his verdict—but he left town without making a commitment.

All along, the question for David had never been

money—it had been whether he wanted to *play* for the Spurs. After they left San Antonio, Lee Fentress talked with his client and David said he needed to think it over for a few days before making a final decision. When they spoke again, David had reached a conclusion.

"From what we've seen of the city," David said, "this is a fantastic place and we love it here."

□

Early in the summer, David had met the press at King's Bay, where he was stationed by the Navy. At that time, he admitted that it wasn't easy living on his Navy salary of $315.23 a week (plus housing), while reiterating his oft-held position that money was not that important to him. When pressed about his feelings concerning the millions that lay in his future, he said, "It's sort of like Christmas, counting down the days waiting until you can open your presents." And he drew a laugh when he responded to a question about what he wanted: "All I want is a guaranteed contract and to be governor within the next ten years."

In a matter of weeks after he authorized Lee Fentress to negotiate on his behalf with the Spurs, it was Christmas ten times over. And if he wasn't guaranteed the governorship, it was about the only thing in his contract that wasn't guaranteed.

From the beginning, everybody wanted the deal done. "The money," according to Spurs' owner Drossos, "was the easy part."

Fentress and the Advantage International team went into the negotiations with Patrick Ewing's guaranteed, multiyear, multimillion dollar contract with the Knicks as their reference point. And despite Drossos's reputation as a skinflint (Jerry Briggs in the *San Antonio Light* called him "the Jack Benny of the NBA"), it was in his bottom-line interest this time to open up the coffers.

Angelo Drossos was not about to lose David Robinson over the issue of a few million dollars. He agreed with Fentress at the very outset that David deserved a deal similar to Ewing's. From there, it was simply a matter of working out the specific points.

David's value to the franchise was incontrovertible:

The Spurs' 1986–87 attendance averaged 8,010 per game. If, with David in the lineup, the attendance increased to an average of 14,000 a game (at sixteen dollars a ticket), revenues would go up by $4.128 million dollars per year, *excluding playoff revenue.* (Actually, the Spurs averaged 14,723 in David's rookie year and 15,769 in his second year. They also enjoyed significant playoff receipts and marketing revenues—and ticket prices rose beyond the average sixteen dollar figure. Thus, the actual increase in revenues, A.D. [after David] exceeded five million dollars a year.)

Another factor Drossos certainly considered in analyzing David's impact was quite simply, *the value of the franchise,* which the owner expected to increase dramatically. In fact, Red McCombs, a minority stockholder in the Spurs at the time of the signing, bought the team in May 1988 (still a year before David would replace his Naval officer's uniform for that of the Spurs) for $47 million, or virtually twice the pre-David assessed value, and estimates of the team's worth at the end of the 1991 season were in the $100 million range.

One of David's strongest negotiating points (along with his basketball talent) was something that just a few months earlier he had thought of as an impediment. David's Naval commitment put him in the unique position of being able to walk away and become a free agent.

McCombs, who at the time was a member of the Spurs' negotiating team, later said, "I think the cards were all stacked on his side of the table. He asked for plenty and he got plenty, what I would call very substantial money. We held the draft rights to him, and there weren't a lot of alternatives for us. What created a conflict for us was the two-year service commitment, and the thought that he could reenter the draft."

The negotiations were extraordinarily rapid. It took only three face-to-face meetings between the two sides to reach an agreement on the complex financial deal. The last meeting, at which the details were hammered out, was a twelve-hour marathon in San Antonio attended by Fentress and Jeff Austin of Advantage and Drossos and McCombs of the Spurs.

Finally, all the *i*'s were dotted and all the *t*'s crossed. It was time to celebrate.

□

On November 6, 1987, David signed a contract with the San Antonio Spurs.

The agreement called for him to receive a million-dollar signing bonus and a million-dollar salary in the first year after signing, plus another million in salary in the second year—all payable before he ever suited up for a Spurs game. To protect his amateur standing, the three million would be placed in a trust fund to be administered by the Amateur Basketball Association of the United States, with a procedure set up for David to draw from the fund.

In each of David's first three active seasons, his salary would be two million dollars a year; this would increase to three million a year for the next three seasons, and would finally peak at four million a year for the last two seasons of the contract. The total value of the package: 26 million dollars for ten years, only eight of which would be playing seasons.

The contract also contained a rather unusual provision: if after the 1991–92 season or at the end of any season thereafter, there are at least two players in the league with a salary of over three million dollars, *and* David had made the NBA all-star team at least twice, *and* he is not among the two top paid players in the league—Robinson can terminate the contract and become a restricted free agent. This provision guarantees, at the very least, that David can renegotiate his contract whenever it falls below the going rate for NBA superstars, in effect giving him a multimillion-dollar cost-of-living escalator.

At a news conference attended by 700 fans, including Mayor Cisneros, David said, "There is no amount of money I would have signed for if I didn't think this team has a commitment to becoming better and to becoming a successful franchise." Later, more than 1,500 people came to the Convention Center

Arena to celebrate his putting pen to paper at a party broadcast live on local TV.

Some people thought it was one of the biggest upsets in modern sports.

Spurs' General Manager Bob Bass crowed, "Nobody thought we would sign him. Nobody. And now, here he is. He's here."

NBA Players Association general counsel Larry Fleischer was genuinely surprised. "I always thought he would wait [two years]. It was just a feeling I had from talking to him a few times."

Most of the league's general managers were thrilled at his decision not to end up with the league's perennials—the Lakers or the Celtics. But Boston's Red Auerbach was shocked: "I'm surprised that he signed with San Antonio. I thought he was going to end up with the Lakers or us. Really. He was in a situation where he did not have to sign with San Antonio, so I thought he would wait it out and say he was going back into next year's draft. If he did that, San Antonio would have to trade his rights or lose everything. At that point, it figured they would trade him to a team that could sign him, which would be the Lakers or us."

But Advantage International's Jeff Austin disagreed. "There was a theory that we could have waited [for him] to become a free agent," he said, "but you're also taking the chance of him being injured or of salary cap problems at some later date. There were a lot of uncertainties with that."

Everything had worked out beyond the Robinson family's wildest dreams. "If you told me a year ago that this would happen, I wouldn't have believed it," remarked David's father, Ambrose. "I wouldn't have believed it six months ago, even two months ago. I manage seventeen million dollars a year in my job—I work with these numbers every day—but this is just unbelievable to me."

Ambrose recalled David's brush with death as an infant and said, "We've felt that David might have been put on this earth for some reason, now this. The Lord certainly does work in mysterious ways."

David's magic touch could not be overestimated. It had been just five years since Art Payne approached the tall transfer student in the halls of Osbourn Park High School, and now the raw kid who hadn't even especially liked basketball had the biggest sports contract in the world. For five years, David had confounded everyone who expected the usual from him; just as his Navy commitment had worked in his favor in the end, so, he felt, would his decision to sign with the Spurs. He would continue to go his own way and make it work for him.

Despite his confidence, there were many people who thought David had passed up a gold mine by not touching down in one of the nation's major media centers. Mike Downey of *The Sporting News* said that if David had signed with LA, Boston, Chicago, or New York, "He could have owned a piece of one of the great cities of Western civilization and been up to his eyeballs in endorsements to boot. With the Spurs, he'll be lucky to do commercials for armadillo food."

But David Robinson didn't care. He owned little San Antonio lock, stock, and barrel. He was the savior in waiting.

"Bird and Michael Jordan," he told the people of his future home, "you don't ever think about how much they're making. You look at Michael Jordan and he should be the top-paid player in the league, all of the things he does, the fans he brings in.

"Hopefully, I'll be able to go on the court and do something similar to that. I'm not Michael Jordan . . . but I am David Robinson, you know."

CHAPTER X

IN DRYDOCK

When he was still a Midshipman First Class, David, like every other middie, had his "wish list" of assignments for the months and years after graduation. Because of his height, he knew he would be on restricted line duty, which meant that he couldn't serve on a sub, fly a plane, or command a Marine unit. But that had been all right with him, because in January 1987 the most important aspect of his life was basketball, and his principal concern in choosing a specialty was that he be assigned to a unit that could allow him to combine his active duty with playing in the NBA.

David and his family examined his choices, and finally settled on the Civil Engineering Corps as the assignment most likely to keep him on the court. The CEC had an initial indoctrination period of only twelve weeks, so if the Navy cooperated, David thought he could get his commission, clarify his status in the NBA, and finish his training before the start of the next basketball season.

Of course all David's planning was rendered

meaningless when Navy Secretary James Webb over-
turned his predecessor on the question of "special
accommodations" for officer-athletes. In the face of
the new policy, it was futile for David to think of
playing organized basketball, except on national
teams in the Pan American and Olympic Games.

Still, David had reached a point where he
thought speech was more effective than silence in
getting what he wanted. He was already banned from
the NBA for two years, and it was unlikely that the
Naval authorities would be so vindictive—and so in-
sensitive to public relations matters—as to punish
him by increasing his commitment. He had nothing
to lose, so he spoke out about what he wanted—and
it wasn't the Olympics. "I've already played against
the best amateur teams in the world and we won the
whole thing," he told *Sports Illustrated*. "I figure I've
done that now. Last year, I was up in the air about
the pros, but yes, I want to play now . . . What I do
best is play basketball and the Navy isn't going to get
the best out of me sitting behind a desk somewhere."

On its part, the Navy was willing to make all the
concessions in the world for David to play basketball
—as long as the arena was "amateur." The brass had
no problems delaying his training-indoctrination session, originally scheduled at the Navy Civil Engineering School in July and August at Port Hueneme, in
Oxnard, California, until after the Pan Am Games.

They also gave him time off-base to make public
appearances, accept awards, meet with dignitaries,
and do whatever else his status as the Navy's most
celebrated ensign required. And long after most of
his classmates had accepted their new commissions

and reported for duty as junior officers, David was still a public figure, with his scheduled arrival at the King's Bay submarine base in Georgia postponed until July.

On June 17, 1987, David appeared as the keynote speaker at Osbourn Park High School's graduation in Manassas, Virginia. He was invited to speak at his alma mater, according to a school spokesman, because of "the students' adoration for him and his position as a perfect role model . . . He is the perfect example to show what someone can make of himself if he puts forth a little bit of effort and develops his untapped talents."

He was all potential, the dream of NBA general managers and advertising agencies alike. He was acclaimed, well known, almost universally respected, a hero to the young, in many ways quite privileged, and not yet rich. He was like a man who reads the winning numbers on his state lotto ticket but can't get to the redemption center. A man on the verge.

One afternoon in late June, the contradictions of his status stood out in bold relief. The previous day he had chatted with George Bush at the White House, golfed for charity with Bob Hope and Tip O'Neill, and been selected by the Spurs as the NBA's top draft choice. He was on top of the world, except he still had only five dollars in his pocket. Just twenty-four hours after his brunch with the Vice President, he went into a Pizza Hut in northern Virginia to order lunch and realized he couldn't afford to buy a soda to go along with his pizza. "Two little girls —one had Pepsi, one had Slice—were sitting there looking at me while I'm looking at my water. It's not cool not to have any money," David said. "Not cool at all."

□

Although it was just a matter of time before he was richer than Croesus, from the moment he arrived at King's Bay in early July, David Robinson was, along with every officer, sailor, and civilian employee on the still-in-construction base, just another working stiff.

His active duty did not begin auspiciously. In the extreme southeast corner of Georgia, where the base was located, the summer of 1987 was stiflingly hot and humid; the air hung heavy over King's Bay's construction sites, and the rain, which arrived virtually every day like clockwork, did little to provide even temporary relief from the oppressive heat.

One afternoon, when the temperature soared well over 100 degrees and the air was saturated with moisture, David drove over to the dock where he checked out the progress of a construction project. When he got back into his air-conditioned car and headed in the direction of his air-conditioned office, he was more than a little relieved. But then he got a flat. Opening the door, the oversized ensign unfolded his long legs out of the driver's seat, felt a blast of steamy air, and cursed the fates that had brought him to such a godforsaken place. As he struggled to change the tire, he grew ever more frustrated and fed up; by the time he got back to his office he was exhausted and soaked through with sweat.

David's problem was not just physical; at King's Bay, David distinctly felt like a fish out of water.

"Here I was this single guy from the north in a small southern town that has nothing in it except one movie house," he said. "It could have been a nightmare." David could sense that people were waiting for him, a famous, 7-foot-tall black man, to go on an ego trip or prove in some other way that he didn't belong. "But I worked hard to establish myself and to do well at my job," he explained. "I wanted to gain the respect of the people at King's Bay." And before long, his efforts paid off, as people began "inviting me to their homes."

David worked from eight in the morning to four-thirty in the afternoon. His primary responsibility was to oversee the steel girder construction of a 145-foot-tall, $35-million, garagelike steel wharf for loading Trident II missiles onto subs. Although he frequently left the office to conduct on-site inspections of construction sites, his was primarily a desk job. He participated in negotiations with contractors and dealt with mountains of paperwork on a daily basis.

Ensign Robinson was part of a team that was putting together the largest peacetime construction project in Navy history. The $1.3-billion King's Bay project, located in the town of St. Mary's, in Georgia's coastal marshes just north of Jacksonville, Florida, would one day be the principal facility for nuclear submarines on the East Coast. The base Commander, Frank Evans, proudly said, "We're spending $800,000 a day building this base. This will probably be the jewel of the Navy." And while Ensign David Robinson toiled in anonymity, a thousand miles away in San Antonio, Spurs' owner Angelo

Drossos and his partners were preparing to spend what must have seemed to them to be almost as many millions on the ensign, the man they considered the future crown jewel of their franchise.

David actually wasn't quite anonymous. Although he said, "You can't live in the limelight your whole life," and described King's Bay as "a place to come and be normal," the spotlight still found him out there in the marshes in the middle of nowhere.

On July 15th, two busloads of media people— reporters, photographers, and TV news crews—piled out into the parking lot in front of the Administration Building at the base. Witnessing the spectacle from inside the building, Navy employees stared out the windows and shook their heads.

Inside, the 21-year-old focus of their attention, resplendent in dress whites, told the assembled multitude, "Frankly, I didn't know that many people were interested in what I was doing down here."

As the cameras rolled and the reporters hunched over their notebooks, Ensign David Robinson carefully avoided criticizing his employer, and made it clear that he was trying to make the best of a situation he would have preferred not to be in. "Every day is something different," he said. "It's exciting. There's so much going on. It's the kind of job where you step in and feel lost because there's so much going on."

David spoke about the specifics of his job, and explained that he was treated no differently from any other junior officer on the base. He said, "Here they tell me, 'You wrote that letter wrong. Write it again, and again, and again,' like they did last week."

When he was asked about his profession in waiting, and about the still controversial decision regarding his status as a basketball player, he said, "I know I have a lot of potential. I don't think that two years is enough, even if I sat around and watched TV all the time, to make me bad enough that I wouldn't make an impact on an NBA team."

He was asked if he had a chance to play any basketball at King's Bay. No, not really, he replied. The only hoops action he could find was in pickup games with sailors who came off the subs. "They all want to dunk over David Robinson," he said. "But I can't let 'em. Not on me."

One of David's supervisors, Commander Fred Clements, also faced the press, saying, "There are a few people who ask for his autograph, but I think most people are trying to just accept him as a Navy person who's trying to do his job. I think people are going out of their way not to be in awe of him."

Less than a week after the buses left the base and the reporters filed their stories, fifty-three more journalists arrived at King's Bay for another go-round. The press simply couldn't get enough of the young officer.

☐

Despite the Navy's attempts to portray Ensign Robinson as just another junior officer, in many ways his life was quite different from most of his peers. While another civil engineer at King's Bay may have found himself looking forward to an occasional weekend in Jacksonville (only one hour south of the base) and a rare, extended leave to visit family or friends, David barely had time to settle in before he was on the move again.

First, the Navy did everything they could to accommodate his plans to play in the Pan American Games in Indianapolis in August. Less than a month after his arrival at King's Bay he was in Louisville working out with the American team. Even though he would have preferred competing in the pros, he accepted the responsibility of representing his country and looked forward to getting back on the hardwood against the best amateurs in the Western hemisphere.

David also used a weekend leave in mid-September to visit San Antonio as the guest of Spurs' management. And after he signed a Spurs' contract, his pocket money rose significantly beyond the $950 a month he took home from his job with the Navy, the amount approved by amateur authorities.

But despite the extra cash, in the fall of '87 Ensign Robinson finally settled into daily life at King's Bay. For David, who had never before been so far from his family and friends, it remained a lonely existence. The press still came around, but it was nothing like the circus atmosphere of his first few weeks at the base.

Soon after the NBA season began in early November he told the *Richmond Times-Dispatch*, "This is kind of tough. I see all my friends starting up with their pro teams and I have nowhere to go. This is a good job, but the place leaves a little to be desired."

He did, however, enjoy a little more leeway than most of his fellow sailors. The money he drew from his future pro team enabled him to buy a new BMW and move into an off-base condo facing the ninth hole of a golf course on Amelia Island, Florida.

Still, he couldn't help but daydream about what he might have been doing and what kind of life he might have been living had he decided to leave the Naval Academy after his sophomore year. But that was all water under the bridge; there was nothing he could do about it now.

After the Pan Am games, David tried to work out on his own, but he knew that without coaching and competition, his game would suffer. Recognizing his need to get on the court with good players, David volunteered to become a part-time assistant coach at Jacksonville University. It was worth driving down to the campus to be able to scrimmage against relatively competitive college ball players on weekends.

At the time, there was still speculation about a possible change in David's commitment to one year. But Commander Mark Neuhart, speaking for Navy Secretary Webb, squelched the rumors by saying, "That's wishful thinking on their part. There's been absolutely no change." And David said he was not interested in asking the Navy to decrease his active duty commitment. "I like my job," he insisted.

In January, David was assigned for indoctrination and training at the Port Hueneme Civil Engineering Corps Officers School in Oxnard, California, a small industrial city just north of Los Angeles. While at school, David lived right along the coast. There was a lot more to do in southern California than there had been in south Georgia. He could head down to the Forum and watch the Lakers play. He could listen to Grover Washington on his stereo and smell the salt breeze. He could work out on the beach as the sun set over the Pacific (an option he reconsidered after being attacked by a chihuahua). But mostly, his time at Port Hueneme was spent in all-day classes. But he wasn't studying something interesting here, like advanced programming or partial differential equations. In an unguarded moment, he confided that while "the teacher's talking about things like cement and concrete, I'm either falling asleep or daydreaming."

Although he was nominally still based at King's Bay, David didn't return to Georgia after finishing Civil Engineering School. Instead, at the urging of amateur basketball officials (who hoped he could get into "reasonable shape" for the Olympic trials in May and the Summer games in September), he reported to the giant Marine base at Camp Lejeune, North Carolina, to join the Navy team in the Armed Forces Tournament.

Almost a year to the day after his brilliant 50-point NCAA performance against Michigan, David suited up in a Navy uniform again to compete against the best players in the Army, Marines, and Air Force. It was nice to see his old friend and nemesis Kevin Houston still shooting his outside bombs for Army. (Houston joked, "Everytime we beat them, they bring in someone new. First it was Kylor Whitaker. Then it was Vernon Butler. Now they're really worried so they brought David back.") There were other good players too, although none close to the level of the best college athletes, much less those in the NBA or international stars like Sabonis.

Naturally, the press and USA Basketball officials

in attendance at the musty old Camp Lejeune fieldhouse had eyes only for David. Even though he hadn't played since the summer, they had every reason to expect that he would dominate the competition. And because he was undoubtedly rusty, they hoped the interservice competition would also prove to be a good test for him. They were stunned by what they saw.

Ensign Robinson did not dominate the Armed Forces Tournament. Against the Army he never got into the flow, scoring just 6 points before fouling out as the Navy was routed 118-71 (giving Kevin Houston a very small measure of revenge for all the losses the Cadets suffered to Robinson and the Middies in their years together at the service academies). David fouled out again in a Navy loss to the Air Force, 95-89, scoring just 17. The only contest in which he was clearly the best player on the floor was in a matchup against the Marines, where he led the Navy to a 134-86 massacre.

The long winter of inactivity had seriously eroded David's basketball skills. He was out of shape, his timing was off, and he clearly had a long way to go before he could compete again against world class competition. If he was going to be any factor at all in the Olympics, he would need to start concentrating on his basketball right away.

Instead of going back to work as a civil engineer at King's Bay, David returned to Annapolis to work his way into shape for the Olympic trials. At Halsey, the scene of so many triumphs, he started a crash training and fitness program—running wind sprints and long distances, swimming and weight lifting and playing pickup ball for four to five hours each day.

David would look up at the empty seats in the old gym and remember the cheers of the crowd. He missed the feeling, and wanted it back. Navy coach Pete Herrmann sympathized with the 1987 Player of the Year's struggle to get back into shape. "The loneliness is difficult for David," he remarked. "This is like a prize fighter training alone to regain his confidence."

David took a break from his solitary regimen to join the U.S. Armed Forces All-Stars in Colorado Springs for an eight-team amateur basketball tournament in mid-April; then he returned to Annapolis. He was exhausted and demoralized, saying, "Sometimes I wish I could just take three weeks off and do nothing."

Unfortunately, there was no time. The Olympic trials were just around the corner, and he still had to show Coach John Thompson that he had the will—and the skill—to come back from his year in drydock and make the team.

CHAPTER XI

PLAYING FOR AMERICA

Twelve months earlier, he had much less to prove. He'd just completed his final college season, and was acknowledged by everyone to be head and shoulders above every other amateur basketball player in the country.

In May of 1987, when the U.S. Pan American team tryouts were held in Colorado Springs, there was no question in Coach Denny Crum's mind about the identity of his starting center. In fact he was so sure about David that he gave him special permission to miss the sessions.

Crum had a host of other talented players to choose from, but he decided to build his squad, not around the twelve best, but around the two best. He felt his linchpins—David and 6-11 forward Danny Manning of Kansas—would be most effectively complemented by a group of athletic and versatile role players who were willing to accept supporting roles. Not everybody can be the main man, the coach reasoned. "After all, this is a team game."

In the middle of July, Crum's handpicked team

joined him at his home base in Louisville, Kentucky. Eleven men came ready to play, fresh from shooting hoops, working out, and playing pickup ball in places like Lexington, Bloomington, Lawrence, and Chapel Hill. The twelfth man—his legs a little stiff and his game a little rusty from sitting behind a desk—came up from King's Bay Naval Base in Georgia. In less than a month all twelve would head up I-65, past soybean crops and Hoosier truck stops, two hours north to Indianapolis where they would compete for the gold against the best amateur basketball players in the Western hemisphere. But first they had to be molded into a team.

With so little time available to prepare, Crum called two-a-day practices. The players were on the court from 9 to 11:30 in the morning and then again from 7 to 9 at night. It was monotonous to run the same offensive and defensive drills over and over again, but the team had to get used to playing to-gether, and they had to learn Crum's up-tempo sys-tem and man-to-man defense.

The two keys to the offense were scoring points in transition and getting the ball into the low post to Crum's main man, Ensign Robinson. Although David wasn't expected to score the way he had at Navy (this time he had much more firepower in his supporting cast), the coach still wanted him to handle the ball where he could use his quickness and size to do the most damage.

Defense was more of an adjustment. Although Crum later said David had the quickness and ability to be as good on defense as anyone, he had very little experience playing man-to-man. Because his college teams never had the pure physical talent to match up, his coaches had always used zones. David worked hard in practice on learning the fundamentals, but he just didn't have the time to catch up.

The boredom of practice was finally broken by a series of exhibition games against NBA pickup squads. The team was impressive, more than holding its own against the pro stars, but most impressive of all was David. He averaged 18.6 points and 9 rebounds a game in the series. And while the centers he matched up against spoke about his great potential, other players were more effusive. Indiana's Scott Skiles called him "a franchise player," and Isiah Thomas pronounced his verdict: "He's something else. He ain't no joke."

By the time the Pan Am games began it was generally assumed that Crum's team would outclass the competition. Despite their youth (all but David were underclassmen), their lack of familiarity with international rules, and the extremely short time they had worked together as a team, the Americans' athleticism and basic abilities, and the fact that they were playing in their own backyard, marked them as prohibitive favorites.

The first round of the basketball competition was set up in two divisions, with each nation playing every other team in its group, and the top two in each division advancing to the medal round.

In the Americans' tournament opener, the Panamanian defense sagged inside against David, who managed to touch the ball only three times in the first half. He finished with just 11 points and 11 rebounds, but the U.S. still came through with an impressive 91-63 victory.

The next time out, against Argentina, David was again far from dominant, shooting just 3 for 9 from the field for 10 points while grabbing 7 rebounds in 20 minutes of action. Again however, the U.S. dominated, winning by an 85-58 margin.

After the American team's third game, a 105-73 rout of Mexico, everybody was wondering where the real David Robinson had gone. Once again, America's main man was invisible. He rebounded well (but then again, so did all the Americans—the U.S. margin off the boards was 51-21 for the game). But he was not a force on offense—he scored only 12 points and never took charge, even when the U.S. trailed 26-24 late in the first half.

Against Venezuela the United States took a 15-0 lead in the first five minutes. If it had been boxing they would have called it a first-round TKO. And David finally had a good all-around game, scoring 17, pulling down 11 boards, and blocking 4 shots in a 109-74 rout.

But the next game, against Uruguay, was nothing short of embarrassing. David fouled out in just 9 minutes of action, scoring 8 points and grabbing only 1 rebound. Nonetheless, it was another U.S. runaway, 105-81.

Going into the semis against Puerto Rico, the Americans appeared all but invincible: they'd won all five of their games by more than 20 points and had an average victory margin of almost 30. But it was clear to everyone, especially Coach Crum, that for the U.S. to continue its dominance in the medal round they'd have to get a more significant contribution from their starting center.

Crum told his team before the semis that they were far from a lock for the gold. Both Puerto Rico and Brazil, the Yanks' likely opponents in the finals, were talented and experienced in international play. Each of the two teams had its own strengths: Puerto Rico had plenty of power down low, with Jose Ortiz, Oregon State's 6-11 Pac-10 Player of the Year and an NBA first-round draft choice leading a contingent of tough, physical, frontline players who were not afraid to mix it up in the paint. Brazil, on the other hand, was famous for its outside gunners, Oscar Schmidt and Marcel Souza, whose mortar shots, when they were falling, could instantly change the complexion of a game. The Americans, Crum explained, should not expect to walk through these two teams as they had the rest of the competition.

One of the coaching staff's biggest concerns going into the semis was keeping David out of foul trouble. They needed him in the game, and knew they could ill afford another debacle like the one against Uruguay. So instead of the natural man-to-man matchup, Robinson on Ortiz, they kept him away from the Puerto Rican big man in the first half.

In one way, the strategy paid off; David played a foul-free half. But on the other hand, it was a disaster. Ortiz went wild, scoring 22 points by intermission on 9 for 12 shooting and leading the Puerto Ricans to a 39-39 tie.

Ortiz had to be stopped. And that, Crum decided, meant switching Robinson into the post on defense while giving him as much weak-side help as possible.

In the first minute of the second half, David showed the Puerto Ricans who owned the paint. As Ortiz went up for his first shot of the period, Robinson went up with him and rejected it. The ball came back to the Puerto Rican post man, and he put it up again. Once again, Robinson's hand was there to block it. A moment later, David was back in the air, controlling the boards after a Puerto Rican miss.

Ortiz ceased to be a factor. With the help of his ball-hawking, double-teaming teammates, David took Jose out of the game, holding the high-scoring big man to a mere two points in the first fifteen minutes of the second half. And on the other end, David was his old dominating self. Whenever the U.S. needed a crucial basket, he was there to get it. With sixteen minutes left, he hit a jumper over Ortiz to give the U.S. a one-point lead. The next time downcourt he electrified the crowd when, after missing a 10-footer, he flew past the Puerto Rican defenders, snared the shot high above the rim, and jammed it home with a shattering slam.

It was exactly what Crum had envisioned. The team was revolving around Robinson and Manning, the two dominant big men, both of whom were moving, shooting, rebounding, and scoring. With six minutes left the coach took his two stars out of the game with the U.S. holding a 72-59 lead. Less than three minutes later the lead was down to 2, Puerto Rico had the ball with a chance to tie, and Robinson and Manning were back in the lineup. After a Puerto Rican turnover, American point guard Pooh Richardson fed David down low and he laid it in for a 4-point lead. The Americans took the game with a final score of 80-75—and the difference was David Robinson. He scored 20, grabbed 13 rebounds, and added 4 blocks, 3 steals, and 2 assists in only twenty-eight minutes of play.

"We haven't needed David to dominate in our other games," said Crum in his postgame press conference. "Today we did, and he was there. We've only been playing him nineteen or twenty minutes per game, and when I can get him twenty-eight or twenty-nine like I did today, he can really do some things out there."

The key for the U.S. in the final against Brazil (which had demolished Mexico, 137-116, in the other semi) was once again to keep David in the game.

On Sunday, August 23rd, playing before a packed house of 16,408 in Indianapolis' Market Square Arena, the U.S. again appeared invincible. For almost twenty minutes, they ran through the Brazilian defense like a hot knife through butter, and despite David's foul trouble (he picked up his third on what he called a "really dumb . . . really bad foul on my part"), they led 66-46 with 54 seconds left in the half.

But the Brazilians weren't finished. In the last seconds, they exploded, cutting the American margin to 68-54 on a 40-foot Marcel Souza three-pointer at the buzzer.

In the first 2:44 of the second half, the U.S. held on. They were leading 76-62 when David jammed home a rebound, felt someone bump his hip, and fearful of being undercut, grabbed the rim momentarily to straighten his body. The whistle blew, and the official pointed at David.

In international rules, hanging on the rim is both a technical and a personal foul. And although the refs had been ignoring the infraction throughout the games, this time they called it. With 17:16 left, David had four fouls; Crum had no choice but to find him a seat on the bench.

Years later, the American Pan Am coach still remembered the basket-hanging ruling. "It was a joke," he said. "There probably wasn't another official in the world who would have made that call."

With David out, the American offense stalled in its tracks. And with the Brazilian sharpshooters Schmidt and Souza bombing from the outside, the lead evaporated. The rim-hanging call gave the momentum to Brazil; within three minutes the South Americans cut ten points off the U.S. margin and in just over six minutes they tied the game, outscoring the U.S. 21 to 5.

Just about everything Schmidt put up went in, and there was nobody on the American team who could keep him from shooting the ball. At one point, with the U.S. still leading 81-77, "The Fabulous Oscar" hit four straight treys for the Brazilians, turning the 4-point deficit into a 4-point lead.

When David returned with 7:41 left, Brazil was up by a point and Schmidt had scored 23 points in his absence. Barely a minute and a half later, Souza drove for the hoop and David cut him off. The whistle blew and David Robinson was out of the game.

"There was no contact at all on the play," said

David. "None, except I might have gotten a piece of the ball." Nonetheless, he was gone. And with him went the American hope for the gold medal.

As he sat on the bench and watched his teammates lose, David felt helpless. While he was in the contest, he had dominated it. He scored 20 points and grabbed 10 rebounds. But he had only played fifteen minutes. Now, in his absence, it was Schmidt's game. While the cold-shooting U.S. squad unraveled, hitting just 16 for 46 from the floor in the second half, the Fabulous Oscar scored 35 points.

At the final buzzer, the score was 120-115. Brazil had pulled off the biggest basketball upset in the history of the Pan American Games. As the Americans sat silently on their bench in stunned disbelief, the Brazilian players pounded each other on the back, jumped on top of each other, and wept for joy.

With tears in his eyes, Oscar Schmidt savored the sweetness of the victory and called it the greatest moment of his life. He said he doubted whether Brazil would have had a chance had Robinson played even twenty-five minutes. But that was little consolation to the young American ensign who had shown such brilliance during his few brief moments on the floor.

A few days later, the final installment of David's Pan Am diary appeared in *The Washington Post*. It was, he wrote, "especially difficult to deal with this defeat." But his concluding thoughts pointed to the future. "When Coach John Thompson assembles his Olympic team," he wrote, "teeth will be a little more tightly clenched and stares will be a little more straight-ahead. . . . I'm already looking forward to the Olympics. We'll bounce back."

For American basketball, and particularly for David Robinson, there was nothing to do but repeat the old Brooklyn Dodger refrain: "wait 'til next year."

□

When David participated in the Armed Forces Tourney in March 1988, Olympic basketball coach John Thompson sent one of his assistants, St. Peter's College Athletic Director Bill Stein, to take a look at the player who was expected to be the leader of his Olympic squad. Stein was alarmed by what he saw: David was tentative, unable to dominate much smaller players who were far from the world-class athletes of the Olympic games. But worst of all was David's inability to run the floor. After just a couple of minutes on the court, the ensign was winded. The desk job had taken its toll, and he was woefully out of shape.

Suddenly there was a question—not only about whether he would be the anchor of the Olympic team —but whether he'd make it at all. And in David's next competition, as a member of the Armed Forces All-Stars in the AAU tourney, he did play better. But he still ran out of gas. The anchor was rusty.

David was still confident that he'd win a place on the Olympic team. But John Thompson, whose style of play placed a premium on physical conditioning, was not so sure.

While the Navy adjusted David's duty to accommodate his need to get back into shape, Thompson summoned the young officer to Georgetown for a talk. It was not a time for assurance. Thompson made it clear that Robinson would have to work to earn his way onto the team—he would not be given a place on the squad on his reputation alone.

The coach questioned the ensign's desire. Did he want a gold medal badly enough to work his way back, he was asked. Did he have the competitive fire to raise the level of his game?

David responded in the affirmative. He was motivated, he said. And he would be ready.

David returned to the Naval Academy, to Halsey Fieldhouse, to work his way back into shape. For the first time he knew with utmost certainty that he would not make the team if he couldn't run up and down the floor. And it was up to him, and the Academy's athletic staff, to make sure he could.

The Navy coaches immediately put David on a crash conditioning program custom-designed to build his endurance and strength. Each day he ran, alternating speed work with distances. He loosened up with swimming. His weight training, overseen by Navy strength coach Steve Murdock, combined free weight and Nautilus workouts. "I believe in working on the entire body instead of just one area or another," explained Murdock. "I have David doing squats to work on the explosiveness of his jump. We are doing a lot more intensive work on his upper body strength." And each day he scrimmaged against the Middies' top big men and Danny Ferry of Duke, who was from Annapolis.

Conditioning became David's single-minded pursuit. And while the Navy didn't simply let him drop everything to get ready to play again, they did modify his duties—he was now working in public relations for his employer instead of sitting behind a desk nine hours a day. And after each appearance at a high school or on a radio talk show to deliver a message of "saying no to drugs and yes to the Navy," he returned to Halsey to work out.

But it wasn't easy. Even with his highly developed sense of Navy discipline, there were times he felt like walking away from the grueling, lonely routine. Still he kept at it day after day, the reason for his tunnel vision never far from the surface. "If you want to play basketball at this level," David knew, "that's all you can do."

John Thompson was aware of how hard his center was working. Whenever he was asked about the state of Robinson's mind and body, he replied that "David Robinson is not a major concern of mine, because I think he is old enough and mature enough to understand what he wants to do and strive toward achieving that."

As the Olympic trials approached and David became more confident about his physical condition, he also became less afraid to openly discuss the Thompson system. "Coach Thompson doesn't emphasize one player. I remember watching him with Pat Ewing, and maybe I'll play that role," he said, before concluding ambiguously, "Obviously, I'm not the player Pat is."

"I'm surprised they remembered me," remarked David when he arrived at the trials in Colorado Springs on May 18th. But he was a presence, playing far better than anyone expected. The other players spoke about the high level of the ensign's game, and even Thompson praised him. Needless to say, David made the first cut.

Still the coaching staff felt he needed real-game experience to get back into competitive trim. To give the ex-Player of the Year a chance to get to work under game conditions, they hastily assembled a Select Team of U.S. players and scheduled a series of exhibitions against European teams in June.

Even though the Select Team's tour of Europe was scheduled for David's benefit, he spent much of the time, according to *USA Today,* "rested like an anchor at the end of the bench." He was a complete nonfactor, shooting just 36 percent from the field and scoring in single digits in a majority of games, including an unbelievably low total of 27 in the first four games of the tour.

What was even more of a concern than his performance was his attitude: he simply didn't seem to be putting much effort into the tour. Even his teammates were concerned. Arizona's Steve Kerr, who was himself fighting for a place on the Olympic squad, worried that "Dave's so rusty and yet he doesn't act like he's into the games at all. I don't see how this tour does the rest of us much good, the competition is so ridiculous. But the whole trip was supposed to be for him. That kind of worries us."

The U.S. Select Team coach and Olympic assistant, Southern Cal's George Raveling, was sparing in his words: "David's not been a problem," he said. "He does what he's told."

But doing what he was told was definitely not enough. Once the Select Team returned to the states, the Olympic squad began a month of rigorous two-a-day practices. As the camp went on, the coaches began to openly express their dissatisfaction and concern with Robinson's play. Thompson rode him in practice, calling him Aristotle or Admiral. The coach wanted his players to obey his orders unquestioningly. With him, it was my way or the highway. But the ensign always wanted to know *why*.

While numerous critics questioned David's desire, others pointed to a variety of factors for his lack of inspiration on the court. Some thought the pressure of performing was simply overwhelming to the young man who signed the $26-million contract—and whom nearly everyone expected to be a combination of Superman and Michael Jordan. Others thought the problem was the Georgetown coach's motion offense. David had never learned to do anything other than set up in the low post, and he appeared bewildered by the unfamiliar offense, lost in the constant movement and cutting away from the ball that was the foundation of Thompson's strategy. Every coach he had ever played for, from Paul Evans to Pete Herrmann to Denny Crum, had adjusted his game plan to fit David's skills; now John Thompson was asking him to adjust his skills to fit the game plan.

Whatever the reason, David began to lose his confidence. "I just haven't reached a comfort level," he said. "I know I can do the things they want me to do, I just haven't done them yet."

By the time the Olympic squad went up against a pickup team of NBA stars in a short exhibition series, David's confidence was reeling. He played creditably in the series opener, scoring 12 and snaring 8 boards in a 90-82 victory. But the foul problems that had plagued him a year earlier in the Pan Am games were back; matched up against Patrick Ewing in the paint, he picked up 3 in the first half and 4 altogether in just eighteen minutes. Ewing's was one of the few encouraging voices. The Knicks center and Thompson favorite praised his Olympic counterpart as "very quick, very explosive." He said David "matched up real well in the banging underneath," and predicted that "he'll do real well."

But even though he played decently against Ewing, David struggled in the series as a whole. He fouled early and often (picking up 15 personals in seventy minutes in 4 games), shot poorly, and scored little. And whenever he was on the floor, he heard his coach on the sidelines. "Grab the ball," Thompson yelled. "Get over there . . . Cut the line off!" Thompson pulled his center off the court and openly expressed his unhappiness with his play. In response, David became less aggressive and increasingly more timid.

The Seattle Supersonics' Alton Lister, matched up against David in one game, observed, "He doesn't look like he knows exactly what they're trying to accomplish out there."

And David said, "I'm aware that people expect a lot of me. . . . I'm trying not to let it get to me, but basically it's hard to see what the coaches are driving us to do."

By August 15th, a *Chicago Tribune* writer was led to write about David's "once-wondrous talents atrophied from disuse." The fact was, however, that he was in decent physical condition by the time of the

Olympic trials. But although he was still relatively unschooled in the game, and the layoff had certainly hurt him, he had regressed markedly since the trials. His confidence was drained. Still, Thompson told *The New York Times,* "The year away set David back. How quickly he comes back depends on [him]. . . . He has to do more work."

After a short series of games against the amateur Athletes in Action, it was time to prepare for the Olympics.

□

It was an unhappy team that arrived in Seoul in mid-September. How unhappy, though, was hard to determine, since workouts were closed to the media and the players were reported to be locked in their rooms at the Olympic Village on Thompson's orders. And because the United States was scheduled to play several games before noon, Thompson ordered the team to meet for breakfast at six-thirty and report for practice at nine. Despite the isolation of the players, there was plenty of audible grumbling.

Charles Smith of Pitt criticized the coach, declaring, "Every player in this room has gone through the stage where he felt 'I'm going to get cut.' He [Thompson] doesn't tell you what he wants. He tells you what he wants as a team, but not individually. That gets confusing."

Speaking to the *San Antonio Express-News,* David's future teammate on the Spurs, Willie Anderson, said, "We're not supposed to talk to the press. Coach Thompson has set aside only certain times when we can talk to reporters. I'm sorry."

Of all the unhappy players, the most unhappy of all was probably David Robinson. He was clearly uncomfortable answering questions at a September 16th press conference, choosing his words carefully in a an attempt at diplomacy. "Everywhere you go," David remarked, "you are going to get a coach with a different philosophy. It is a player's job to adjust to a coach."

When asked about his apparent loss of confidence, he replied, "I don't get the ball thirty times in the paint. That doesn't mean I'm not confident, though. I'm as confident as I was before, but I'm confident about playing a different role. I am very, very confident about what I can do for this team. I can rebound, block shots, and intimidate people." For all intents and purposes, he appeared to have given up trying to fit in with the Olympic team's offense.

George Schaefer of the U.S. Navy's Recreation Department spoke to David and told the press, "David said he's had problems with Thompson. It's not a personality thing or anything like that, he just hasn't been able to play that well in Thompson's system.

"Thompson's game is to run and David likes to run, but he also likes to post up and that's something he hasn't been able to do because of Thompson. David said he might be scoring better if he could post up and become more involved in the offense."

Three years after the Olympics, David would be quoted in *Gentleman's Quarterly:* "Thompson was a dictator. You had to go his way. It was always *his* gym, *his* team, *his* this. . . . He wants you scared of him. He degrades you. He told me I couldn't play. I said, 'Okay, that's fine, I can't play.' He didn't understand I could be devoted to the game and still have other interests. He was used to having kids for whom basketball's everything. He gets into your mentality. I just didn't agree with the mind games he plays."

Thompson's response: "All I'll say is it wasn't his role to agree with me. I don't permit people to question me, or else they're not on my team."

☐

Americans always believe they should win in international basketball, but the pressure on the 1988 U.S. Olympic team was even greater than usual. The Soviet Union and the United States had not met in the Olympics since 1976, with the U.S. boycotting the Moscow games in 1980 and the Russians returning the favor in Los Angeles in 1984. The 1984 American five (with Michael Jordan, Patrick Ewing, and a virtual galaxy of future NBA stars) may well have been the greatest amateur basketball team in history, but they were forced to accept a hollow victory when the Eastern bloc refused to join in the competition. The United States had only defeated the Soviets once —in 1976—since the disputed Russian victory in 1972 ended America's unbeaten record in the Olympics. And international basketball had since taken giant steps to catch up to the United States.

The U.S. defeat in the 1987 Pan American games had stunned American basketball officials. It was becoming clear that pickup all-star teams of collegians would be hard-pressed to continue winning against experienced national squads. It also seemed to John

Thompson and other American amateur authorities that the increasing internationalization of the NBA gave aid and comfort to the enemy. (NBA teams like the Atlanta Hawks and the Milwaukee Bucks scheduled games against the Soviet national squad. And the Portland Trail Blazers, who had drafted the U.S.S.R.'s star center Arvidas Sabonis, brought him to the United States to rehabilitate his injured Achilles tendon.)

Coach Thompson and U.S. Olympic Committee and ABA-USA officials began speaking openly about bringing NBA players into the 1992 Olympics, in order to tilt the playing field in favor of the United States once again. There was little question that this would be the last Olympics for American college stars. Particularly if the kids didn't win.

And the atmosphere of discontent did nothing to help their chances.

□

The U.S. team tipped off its action against an overmatched Spanish squad. It was a 97-53 United States rout—and David was as dominant as ever with a game-high 16 points, 11 rebounds, and 4 blocks.

The next day, though, it became abundantly clear that this competition would not be a walkover. Playing against Canada, the United States struggled throughout the game with foul trouble. David picked up his second with 15:10 left in the first half and was pulled by the coach until after intermission. The Americans finally managed to defeat the pesky Canadians 76-70 as David blocked 5 shots, but managed to score only 4 points.

There was no rest for the weary American team. The next day they played Brazil, the team that had beaten an American squad just one year earlier to win the Pan Am Games. This time though, the United States won, 102-87, despite more early foul trouble for David that contributed to his anemic stat line of 11 points, 2 rebounds, and 2 blocks.

In a postgame press conference, David responded testily to a question about how he was adjusting to Thompson: "Those questions are so stupid," he snapped. "Why don't you look at the game? What do you expect me to do? Take 20 shots a game?

"Why don't you ask Coach Thompson if he is upset with the way I've been playing. He isn't and as long as he's not, I feel okay."

By now, questions about Thompson's personnel choices, which had surfaced as far back as the Olympic trials in Colorado Springs, were rampant. Considering the international game's emphasis on the three-point shot, why was Hersey Hawkins the only true outside threat? And despite their hard-nosed defensive talents, weren't there better all-around point guards than Virginia Tech's Bimbo Coles and Georgetown's Charles Smith?

The Americans' easy 108-57 victory over China (who had only one player taller than 6-3) answered none of the nagging questions, and even brought up a few more, as both Hersey Hawkins and swing man Willie Anderson were injured, joining backup center J. R. Reid and defensive specialist Stacey Augmon on the sidelines. When the U.S. finished its preliminary round play undefeated with an easy victory over

Egypt, no one was convinced of the Americans' invulnerability.

Soon there were only four teams left in the competition. And with the Soviet Union up next against the United States, there would be no more breathers.

The Russian team was essentially the same squad that had lost to a different group of young Americans in the 1986 World Championships, when David, then a Navy undergraduate, held off Arvidas Sabonis and the United States held on for a 2-point win.

This time around, David reintroduced himself to the big Soviet center soon after the opening tap, when he stuffed the Russian bear in the very first minute of play. But despite David's emphatic greeting, it was the Russians who took the early lead. Playing a disciplined, patterned half-court offense, they frustrated the American transition game and denied the quicker, more athletic U.S. squad any opportunities to run. After the first two minutes, the Americans were relegated to playing catch-up.

Early in the first half, Danny Manning, who had been a one-man gang in leading the Kansas Jayhawks to an NCAA title, picked up his second foul and took a seat on the bench. He never did get back into the flow, and was shut out. The savvy and experienced Soviet guards, meanwhile, took the air out of the ball; they worked it around for the best possible shot on almost every possession, got back on defense, and forced the run-hungry Americans to walk the ball upcourt. The one matchup the United States was clearly winning was at center—at least when Robinson was in the game.

Despite the Russians' ability to control the

tempo, the Americans managed to stay close through much of the first half. When David hooked in a 2-pointer to tie the score at 27, NBC's Al McGuire (who years earlier had dubbed then-Midshipman Robinson "Navy's aircraft carrier") commented that his play "justifies San Antone" and its massive contract. McGuire's statement was almost a direct response to a *USA Today* column by CBS analyst Billy Packer. "I think David's a nice player," Packer wrote, "but he's not worth $26 million."

Despite Robinson's efforts, the Russians slowly but surely pulled away. By halftime they had a 10-point lead, and the situation appeared desperate. But the American kids had heart, and they wouldn't give up. They fought back, turned up the defensive pressure, and twice closed the gap to 2 in the second half. But whenever they got close, the Soviets regained their composure and refused to panic. They stayed within their game plan, continued to work the ball around, and exploited the American team's weaknesses.

Manning's nonproduction was devastating, but so was the inability of the Americans to open up the defense. The lack of both a legitimate 3-point threat and a strong penetrating point guard meant the Soviets could lay back and clog the middle. And mysteriously, despite early foul trouble for Sabonis, the American guards stopped looking to get the ball into Robinson in the paint.

Many observers also felt that Thompson's substitution pattern, which was designed to bring fresh legs into the action at every opportunity, instead served as a momentum breaker, particularly for those players

—like David Robinson—who take time to get into the rhythm of the game. It almost seemed as if every time the American center started to become a factor he ended up on the bench. He finished with 19 points (on 6-12 from floor and 7-10 from line) while adding 12 rebounds, 2 blocks, and 2 steals—all in just twenty-six minutes of play. But at the end, he was just watching.

In the final minute, a Willie Anderson steal and stuff pulled the United States to within 3. With the game on the line, Thompson went with a small, quick lineup, hoping to force a turnover with defensive pressure. But with no American on the floor taller than 6-7, the Soviets controlled the boards in the waning seconds, and despite missing two shots, they were able to run out the clock. The final score was 82-76, U.S.S.R.

For the second straight year, the United States had come up short in international competition. It was only America's second loss (and first undisputed defeat) in Olympic basketball history. The Russians were on their way to the gold.

The United States, meanwhile, had to be satisfied with defeating Australia, 78-49, to salvage the bronze. For John Thompson and his team, it was no consolation.

For David the loss was particularly galling. Twice in two years he had been America's main man, and twice America had failed to win. And now, while the rest of the squad went back to their colleges or on to the pros, he returned to King's Bay, Georgia, where for one more season he could do nothing but wait and watch—on the sidelines.

CHAPTER XII

THE WAITING GAME

Late in the winter of 1988, Secretary of the Navy James Webb, following in the footsteps of former Secretary John Lehman, resigned his post. The announcement fueled new speculation that after the Olympics, the Navy might release its tallest ensign to play pro basketball. A finalist at the Sullivan Awards banquet in March (honoring the nation's top amateur athlete), David was asked to comment on a possible change in his commitment with the swearing-in of a new Navy Secretary. "It's totally ridiculous to think I'll be out early," he replied. "People in San Antonio better hope he [Navy Secretary-elect William L. Ball III] doesn't come in and change it to five years."

Still, on October 5th, within days of his son's return from the Olympics in Seoul, Ambrose Robinson told the *San Antonio Light* that he was optimistic about an early release. Working with Aldrich Mitchell, David's cousin, the senior Mr. Robinson was reported to have come up with a proposal for the Navy based on four points:

- David's good faith in remaining at the Naval Academy after his sophomore year;
- David's height, which caused him to be excluded from many duties;
- David's potential for public relations service to the Navy as a spokesman and celebrity playing in the NBA;
- An agreement by David to extend his reserve duty commitment.

The next day, Spurs season ticket sales jumped 40 percent, a spokesman for U.S. Senator Phil Gramm reported that the senator would "lobby on San Antonio's behalf," and David's future employers and teammates were ecstatic about the possibilities of Ensign Robinson's active duty on the Spurs.

While David himself could not be reached for comment, his superior officer at King's Bay, Captain Ken Fusch, issued a statement: "Now that the Olympics are over, we have received word to fully expect [Robinson] to be returning to duty here. We haven't heard anything about any petition to change his status with the Navy."

Meanwhile, David's agent, Lee Fentress, had also been working behind the scenes for an early release. But when he contacted the Navy Secretary, he was advised that no request would be considered unless it was made by the ensign himself, and that the request would have to go through the chain of command.

According to regulations, David would have to personally submit a petition for a change of status to his immediate superior officer. The petition would then be reviewed by each succeeding higher ranking officer until it finally reached the desk of the Navy Secretary. Each officer along the way would have the option of either endorsing or opposing the petition, but the final judgment would be the Secretary's alone.

On October 5th, David wrote to Navy Secretary Ball, requesting a release from active duty in exchange for an additional three years in the Naval Reserve. For two weeks, the city of San Antonio held its collective breath. Finally, on October 20th, Secretary Ball rejected the request, declaring that he "would not tamper with Navy policies regarding active-duty servicemen and professional sports endeavors by providing Robinson with a special exemption." It was a dark day in river city.

The local press lambasted Ball, declaring that he had blown the call. *San Antonio Light* sportswriter John Lopez wrote, "Military precision took precedent over . . . reason," and the headline over Buck Harvey's column read, "Navy dropped the Ball . . ." Spurs' majority owner B. J. "Red" McCombs was even more direct. The secretary's decision was "a no-brainer," he said, because a release was not only "logical," the Navy secretary should have been "doing cartwheels because he received such a proposal."

"Getting the word," McCombs added, "was like getting kicked in the stomach by Hulk Hogan."

Despite the feelings of his future employer, David was still in the Navy. And in a statement he released through his agent, he made it perfectly clear that he was still a Navy man. "I am proud to have been allowed to serve in the Navy over the past seventeen months," he said, adding that he was "not trying to avoid a commitment, but rather to increase my commitment if the interests of the Navy could be served by such. I respect the Secretary's decision and look forward to serving the remaining six months on active duty and six years of reserve duty with pride."

A few days later, Jan Hubbard of the *Dallas Morning News,* analyzing the Robinson case, quoted extensively from a General Accounting Office report entitled "Treatment of Prominent Athletes on Active Duty." The document indicated that when David signed his contract for active duty, the language in the standard contract was altered. "The provision requiring Robinson to serve a full two years of active duty under the OSAM (Officers' Sea and Air Mariner) program is inconsistent with other OSAM participants. The OSAM program authorization document states that officers will be released from active duty after completing either two years of active duty *or* the civil engineering officers school, approximately eight weeks in duration . . .

"The standard OSAM contract has a paragraph saying that the participant consents to serve 'on active duty for a period of *up to* two years.' The contract the Navy had Robinson sign omits 'up to.' We were told that these words were omitted to ensure that Robinson would serve for two years. However, according to Robinson, he was told that he would likely be released from active duty after the Olympics."

Despite the revelations, there was no further appeal. David remained in drydock.

□

On the day after Thanksgiving, thousands of San Antonians watched Mayor Henry Cisneros and Ensign David Robinson (who was on leave from the U.S. Navy) join together to throw the switch that illuminated Alamo Plaza's 48-foot blue spruce Christmas tree. Thousands more watched at Rivercenter, San Antonio's giant indoor-outdoor mall, where the two threw a second switch, bathing the pristine, sub-street level River Walk in the shimmering glow of 50,000 electric lights. The illumination started the annual River Parade: with more than 100,000 spectators jamming the banks of the river, the shopping plaza, and nearby hotel balconies, the music flowed nonstop and grand marshal Robinson waved as he floated by on one of the parade's twenty-three floats. (The others were inhabited by King Antonio LXVI, El Rey Feo XL, the Queen of the Gardenia and Musical Club, Mud King and Queen II, the Mayor, Santa Claus, and Santa's cousin Pancho, who flew up from south of the border on his flying burro Chuy to wish all the inhabitants of the historic home of Texas independence a *Feliz Navidad.*)

For the Spurs, however, Christmas would have to wait.

Larry Brown, who had replaced Bob Weiss as coach after leading Kansas to the NCAA championship the previous spring, experienced his first losing year as a coach on any level. Despite the emergence of rookie swingman Willie Anderson as the team's leading scorer, the Spurs were horrendous. They were selfish and undisciplined—pointing fingers and blaming each other for every failure. The team's second leading scorer, former St. John's All-American Walter "The Truth" Berry, complained, "Larry's a fundamentals coach, and I'm not big on fundamentals." Soon thereafter, he became the first casualty in Brown's housecleaning. Other less prominent players also disappeared. The Spurs even began shopping their star guard, defensive specialist Alvin Robertson, who was clearly unhappy with the new coach's style.

As the team sank beyond mediocrity, Coach Brown looked on the bright side. "At least if we don't turn it around," he said, "we'll be a lottery team, and maybe we can get somebody to help us." He could afford to take the long view. Help was already on the way. "You can talk about us struggling all you want," he said with a smile as his Spurs plummeted to a franchise-worst 21-61 record, "but we're a lot different than other teams, because we have David Robinson waiting in the wings."

CHAPTER XIII

SHAKING OFF THE RUST

The waiting was the hardest part. After two interminable years, Lieutenant Junior Grade David Robinson, U.S. Naval *Reserve* finally arrived. Amid great anticipation, David came shortly before ten on a midsummer Saturday morning, to a high school athletic complex on the outskirts of town.

He went beyond the airport, past the suburban houses and malls, past the auto parts stores and fast food restaurants, to Blossom Athletic Center, a mere speck on the horizon when viewed from the top of downtown San Antonio's Tower of the Americas. As he approached the small field house, he saw rows and rows of empty school buses waiting for the new school year in a massive, otherwise abandoned parking lot. He went past the lot—down to street level—to where the coaches and press and Spurs' brass parked. He entered the building as inconspicuously as possible, bending slightly as he passed through the unlocked but guarded back door. He smiled with anticipation as he heard the rhythmic thumping of round balls on hardwood and saw the coaches and the athletes within. He was finally home.

As scheduled, the 1989 San Antonio Spurs' rookie and free agent camp kicked off on Saturday morning July 22nd at Blossom, its usual anonymous site. But for once, the camp was hardly an anonymous affair. David Robinson was ready to be anointed king of the city. The waiting was finally over.

Like all the other NBA summer camps, the Spurs' rookie and free agent camp is serious business. For the athletes who participate, the competition is fierce and injuries common. The players—all of whom were *stars* in college—are in a desperate fight to fill out the last roster spots. For most, sticking with an NBA team means the difference between a year's income of well over $100,000 plus perks (including first-class travel and accommodations), and either giving up the dream of pro ball, or living a gypsy life in the foreign pro leagues, or riding the buses and sleeping in second-rate motels in the CBA for $15,000 a year.

A player who puts on Spurs' silver and black for the four days before the first cuts has to tread a thin line: on the one hand, he needs to burn the man across the court from him one-on-one; on the other, he must learn the plays and show he can fit into Coach Larry Brown's system. Most of the two dozen or so athletes on the court know the odds of sticking with the team are very long and that this trial by fire is just the first phase of the winnowing process. There are just not that many jobs available.

But David was different. He was Davy Crockett, Jim Bowie—the new hero riding in to save the day for the Alamo City. Although summer camp was in many ways as much a learning experience for him as it was for the other players, he was already the Spurs' $26 million man and this was his coming-out party. His job was guaranteed.

Despite all the expectations, David, who hadn't played competitive basketball (outside of a little touring with the Navy All-Stars and all-service teams) since the previous year's Olympic disaster, went into camp with a lot to prove. Would he be as good as he was cracked up to be? Would he be in playing shape? The people of San Antonio hoped and prayed he would be.

□

Lieutenant J.G. David Robinson had officially become a civilian on May 19th, and immediately upon his release from active duty, had started to work with the Spurs on plans for his upcoming rookie season. One of the first orders of business was to greet the fans, who were already putting in their orders for season tickets, thereby adding extra dollars to the coffers of Red McCombs and his partners in anticipation of the heralded rookie's impact on the team's fortunes.

On Sunday, May 21st, David met his public at the arena, answering questions submitted (in writing) by Spurs' boosters.

"Will you buy me a Porsche?" one question read.

Nonplussed, Robinson replied, "Uh, no."

Silence. Why not?

"You see, I went to a Porsche dealer and I found one I really liked. I went to my mom and asked her what she thought about it. I always like to go to my mom on things like that. She said, 'No, you can't have one. They're too fast. You might kill yourself.'

"So," David smiled triumphantly in conclusion, "if I can't have one, you can't either."

Having disposed of the question about distribution of his contract, he turned to other, more pertinent ones—most of which were concerned with how David would earn his money, not spend it.

The fans and front office all wanted to know whether Robinson would still have it—the charismatic force that made him one of the most celebrated college players of the decade. What kind of condition was he in after sitting at a desk for so long? Would he be able to adjust to the pro game? Was he worth *all* that money? And judging by the relatively minor impact in the standings of recent years' #1 draft choice rookie centers (including Olajuwon and Ewing), could he make all that much difference to his team?

By summer camp, the Spurs had done their part, making good on their promise to build a competitive, complementary team around Robinson. They had traded to get All-Star power forward Terry Cummings (unloading disgruntled All-Star guard Alvin Robertson and Greg "Cadillac" Anderson in the process); they had nurtured shooting guard Willie Anderson (and Willie, despite his team-leading 18.6-point per game rookie season and assurance of a spot on the starting five, was on hand at Blossom, ready to join his Olympic and Pan Am Games teammate on the court when he arrived). As Larry Brown had wished while his team sank into the depths the previous season, they'd been rewarded with another lottery pick, and used it to draft (as the number three choice overall) 1989 College Player of the Year Sean Elliott to play small forward. Plus they'd also brought in one of the game's savviest old pros, center Caldwell "Pops" Jones, to teach the rookie the ropes.

□

The Saturday morning session at Blossom was all drills and basic skills—a symposium on repetition run by Professor Brown. The players ran, shot layups, and passed, passed, and passed. They took the ball off the glass and put it back up. They went into a weave, moving from the baseline to the top of the key, taking the pass, and firing it back with two hands toward the hoop to the cutter. They filled the lane on the break, and worked to move their feet on defense. It was a pure, physical statement of basketball fundamentals.

The studious-looking, Brooklyn-born coach patiently ran through the plays, pushing the younger men to the point of exhaustion. All too aware of the significance of the next four days, the players pushed themselves even harder. Winded, breathing hard, they periodically jogged off the court to grab a sip of Gatorade and return for more punishment. And from behind his round, tortoiseshell glasses, Brown carefully watched the action, assessing where each man might fit in as a member of the San Antonio Spurs.

With one man on the court that morning, there was no question. Barring a natural disaster, David Robinson was guaranteed the job as the Spurs' start-

ing center. He would be the center even if he didn't
play well that morning at Blossom. But his performance was better than expected; Brown and his staff
couldn't help but think about him *as* the franchise.

After two hours, the practice ended and the players showered. Most returned to the airport hotel
where the team put them up, to catch a few winks,
prowl the lobby, and watch TV. A few, including the
prize rookie, had better places to go and better things
to do in the few hours between practices. Unlike the
free agents, whose lives were on hold for the duration
of the camp, the rest of David's life was just beginning, and he had a lot of catching up to do.

□

The day's second session was held at dusk. Unlike the
morning grind, it gave the rookies and free agents a
chance to scrimmage, to show what they could do in
a simulated game situation. It was competition, but
at the same time it was still practice.

With David Robinson as the featured attraction,
the Spurs sold this hybrid form of stop-and-go, do-it-
over round ball to a near capacity crowd of 3,500 at
Blossom. The screaming patrons, who compared fa-
vorably in both numbers and enthusiasm to those
who attended *regular season* games at the HemisFair
Arena during the pre-Robinson years, watched as
King David soared and stuffed, attacking aggressively
on both ends of the floor.

Larry Brown was pleased, and despite his warning to the press that his new star would struggle some
during the rookie camp, in the Southern California
Pro League, and in preseason, he said, "He's going to

be everything we hoped for, and I'm thrilled for this whole community, not just the team."

Owner Red McCombs also had a right to exhale deeply; at first glance, his megamillion-dollar investment looked even better on the court than it did on paper. In fact, David was already paying his way, even after the first night of practice.

Everybody was happy.

On Tuesday night, the rookies and free agents suited up for the annual Black and Silver game, pitting two squads against each other in an actual, end-to-end, 48-minute, NBA-style game. It was a spectacular coming out party for David, who dominated the contest as if he'd never been away. Performing in front of a capacity crowd of 4,322, David unleashed a full air assault, rattling the rims with showtime jams, intimidating any opponent foolish enough to venture into the paint, rejecting shots, racing downcourt to finish fast breaks, putting the ball on the floor, and swooping in from the top of the key for stuff city. He finished with 31 points, 17 rebounds, and 10 blocks in thirty-one minutes of action, and left everyone in attendance convinced they had seen the future.

Bob Bass couldn't hide his exuberance. "No big man has ever been like this," he exulted. "Nobody. Name even a 6-foot-9 guy with that quickness. I tell you, James Worthy can't run like David."

Larry Brown was equally effusive. "This far exceeded anything I expected," he said. "[David] was phenomenal."

In analyzing his own performance, David was more laid back and modest. "I feel that I am learning," he said. "I was happy I was able to run the floor and not get tired. But I'm not there yet. I'm still not ready for the Ewings or Olajuwons, but," he concluded, exuding confidence, "I will be."

The next day, David helped celebrate the founding of the San Antonio chapter of the "I Have a Dream Foundation." (Started by New Yorker Eugene Lang in 1981, the foundation guarantees students in inner-city elementary schools full college tuition for everyone who graduates from high school.) He then joined the remaining Spurs' wannabes—among those cut after the Black and Silver game was former Syracuse All-American Pearl Washington—back on the floor at Blossom to play their first game in the Midwest Rookie Revue.

The Revue, a three-day round robin event featuring the rookie and free agent survivors from four NBA camps (the Houston Rockets, Denver Nuggets, and Minnesota Timberwolves joined King David and the Spurs in the 1989 event), opened with the Spurs facing off against the expansion Timberwolves. Those who were expecting greatness every night were disappointed, as David was merely mortal, with 22 points, 6 rebounds and 5 blocks in a close victory. "It's just a matter of me being focused," he said. "I've got to be mentally ready every night."

The following night he was back on track, overwhelming the Houston rookies with 27 points, 9 rebounds, 5 steals, and 3 blocks in twenty-seven minutes. And he was once again *The Force* on the floor in the Spurs' revue finale, leading them past the Nugget rookies with 19 points, 11 rebounds, 5 blocks, and 2 steals in just twenty minutes on the floor. In sweep-

ing through the rookie revue, David left no doubt
that he would immediately begin paying the Spurs
dividends on their investment.

The process of preparing David for the rigors of
his premier NBA season continued two nights later,
when San Antonio's entry in the Los Angeles Summer League tournament tipped-off against a squad of
New York Knick summer temps. In a repeat of his
less-than-spectacular Midwest Revue performance
against the T-Wolves, David seemed to drift. At times
he allowed Eddie Lee Wilkins to push him off the
blocks, and he rarely utilized his superior athletic
skills to take control of the contest.

It was clear to the Spurs that David needed to
prepare himself mentally as well as physically for the
upcoming season. He and Spurs assistant coach
Gregg Popovich talked at length about concentration
and focus, about David's need to maintain his motivation and intensity day after day after day throughout the course of the long NBA campaign. Nobody
questioned his ability to get himself up for a big
game, rather the challenge was to keep the competitive fire going throughout a long road trip in the middle of the season. There were sure to be letdowns;
everyone had them. The point was to minimize them.

The L.A. Summer Pro League was as good a
place as any for David to begin work on the mental
aspect of his game while getting his feet wet in something approaching NBA-level competition. While
most of the top draft picks, the can't-miss prospects
signed to multiyear, multimillion-dollar contracts,
could afford to pass up the summer league, David
needed it—both he and the Spurs' coaching staff

wanted him to play himself back into competitive shape while learning more of the skills he would need to excel as an NBA center.

While in L.A., he faced talented and hungry ball players literally every night. There were veterans and young hotshots trying to recover from injuries and stick in the NBA; low draft choices with an outside shot of making the grade; and journeymen and free agents with borderline major league talent who sometimes appeared to the evaluators of talent to be both eminently disposable and interchangeable. There was five-foot-seven-inch Greg Grant, drafted number 52 by the Suns but given a good chance to make the team because of his speed and penetrating ability; veteran small forward Gene Banks, who had once scored 15 points a game for the Spurs and was now trying to recover from knee surgery and get a second life with the expansion Charlotte Hornets; sharp-shooter Steve Kerr, Sean Elliott's teammate at Arizona who was trying to patch up his battered and bruised body to play for the Suns; and a host of the "enemy," Eastern European Olympians like Yugoslavians Vlade Divac (signed by the Lakers) and Zarko Paspalj (a member of the Spurs) and Russians Sarunas Marciulionis (Golden State) and Alexander Volkov (Atlanta).

But first, standing head and shoulders above the competition, there was Lieutenant J.G. David Robinson, USNR. He was still—he would always be—number 50. Now on active duty with the San Antonio Spurs.

For David it was a brand new experience. "The hardest thing," he said, "is playing so frequently and being up all the time. There are people trying to kill you *every* night. The big guys out there are trying to make a name for themselves. . . . It's definitely not like playing against William & Mary."

The summer league also allowed him to learn more about Larry Brown's passing game, which instead of anchoring him at the low post had him moving between the paint and the top of the key.

He was at his best in the first half against the Sixer rookies at Loyola Marymount, rejecting shots, sinking short jumpers, and appearing for all the world to be a speeding projectile as he filled the lane to finish fast breaks with emphatic slam dunks. He had 28 points at intermission but let down in the second half just enough to allow the Sixers to come back to win.

As the days went on, David made his share of rookie mistakes. And he still had lapses of concentration, but they gradually became more infrequent and were far overshadowed by extended periods of utter dominance.

By the end of the summer league season, David was the Most Valuable Player, with averages of 25.6 points, 6.4 rebounds, and 4.2 blocked shots per game.

□

Back in San Antonio, the Spurs' new center approached his task with single-minded dedication. Each day he went to the state-of-the-art Concorde Athletic Club, where he worked out for five hours—combining Nautilus, Stairmaster, and free weight workouts with squash, basketball, stretching, and running. By the time preseason practice began, David was in the best physical condition of his life.

Larry Brown and Gregg Popovich also went one on one with their star pupil. They discussed strategy with him, explained his role on the team, and continued to stress his mental preparation for the long season ahead.

Pulling out all the psychological stops, Brown even invited Navy Coach Pete Herrmann to San Antonio with the hope of gaining more insight into Robinson's personality. Brown knew all about David's diversity of interests—he'd seen him playing his grand piano and was aware that he'd recently begun to study Spanish and comparative theology—and he wanted to be sure to motivate the Spurs' renaissance man to do it all *on the basketball court.* Herrmann did his part; after he visited David at home, the rookie found October 6th (the first day of preseason camp) circled on his calendar and marked with the words, "Get ready to go with the big boys."

Meanwhile, Brown and Bob Bass were completing their housecleaning. After the summer league, the Spurs traded their young point guard Johnny Dawkins for the unflappable veteran Maurice Cheeks. By training camp, there were only three Spurs remaining from the 1988–89 season—Willie Anderson, Frank Brickowski, and Vernon Maxwell. And when Sean Elliott finally agreed to terms in October and joined the team in camp, the starting five was set: Cheeks and Anderson at the guards, Elliott and Cummings at forward, and Robinson at center.

The situation was perfect for David. For him, it was the Middies all over again, but on a higher level.

The Spurs, with four new players (including two rookies) on their starting five, had nothing to prove and everything to gain. The team was bound to get better, but nobody was openly predicting that they'd be among the biggest winners in the league. A five hundred record would suffice for most fans after the futility of the previous few years.

David also had a coach, in Larry Brown, who pushed him in much the same way as Paul Evans had done. "Man, Coach Brown is always on me," he told the *Los Angeles Times.* "You can go out and score 40 points and he'll be furious about a thousand other things. A lot of people can't understand someone yelling at them all the time, but I need that. I don't need someone to pat me on the back." Brown, like Evans, not only yelled at David; he also protected him and made sure he learned what he needed to know to "go with the big boys."

With Caldwell Jones as a personal mentor, David began to pick up some of the fine points of post play in the NBA. Although he was still relatively untutored at his position, his natural talent and intelligence made an immediate impression on the grizzled 39-year-old veteran. Just a day after practice began, Jones had already seen enough to exclaim, "Whatever they're paying him, he's worth it."

As the Spurs began to get into the exhibition schedule, it became clear to NBA insiders that this was a team to reckon with, not just in the future, but perhaps in the present too. David was adjusting rapidly, showing that he could more than hold his own against the league's centers. He even played the Knicks' Patrick Ewing to a standoff in Madison

Square Garden. After the game, Ewing was already acknowledging that a new star had arrived in the NBA.

"People will always compare us," said Ewing. "It's like comparing me and Hakeem . . . Tonight [Robinson] did an outstanding job. He's very quick, and agile, and he's very smooth with his footwork. He can play."

By the time November rolled around and the regular season began, David and the Spurs were ready for anything. Management's franchise-building strategy was about to pay off, and a new era in the team's history was about to begin.

Caldwell Jones, who knew his own days in the NBA were soon to come to an end, looked at the future and declared, "He's going to be a force in this league for a long time."

CHAPTER XIV

MR. ROBINSON'S NEIGHBORHOOD

On the evening of November 4, 1989, by the time David Robinson drove past the kids clamoring for his autograph and into the players' gate of San Antonio's HemisFair Arena, there was already a buzz of electricity outside in the plaza.

Everybody in the Alamo City was talking about him: the drivers of Riverwalk tourist boats discussed him as they deposited their passengers back at the Marriott; his name was whispered by the Daughters of the Texas Republic in the rough-hewn stone shrine to Crockett, Bowie, and the rest of the heroes of the old Mission San Antonio de Valero; it was shouted outside the convention center above the dull thunder of silver-flecked Air Force fighter jets—and most likely by the pilots in the cockpits as well.

His potential was analyzed by shoppers in the ultramodern multilevel Rivercenter mall, and predictions about his impact were made next door over gin and tonics in the sedate, old-world bar of the nineteenth-century Menger Hotel. Tourists riding the elevator to the top of the Tower of the Americas watched the crowd gathering in front of the arena and wondered what the fuss was about. But natives spoke of him as a long-lost relative come home. He was the man of the hour on Paseo Del Rio, Market Street, Commerce, and even in Ripley's Believe It Or Not.

The city had been waiting for David for two long years. Now he was finally about to make his official debut as a Spur in the season opener at the Hemis-Fair, against Magic Johnson and the Los Angeles Lakers.

As David walked past the guards into the sports center's offcourt staging area, he acknowledged their best wishes and felt some butterflies as he turned left and strode into the Spurs' locker room. When he sat, his leg moved up and down like a piston at a hundred miles an hour. He couldn't wait for the game to start.

By the time he took the court for the pregame warm-ups, the purple seats set back from the court were nearly full and people were still filing in, filling every seat in the auditorium. With the presence of the national media, press row was more crowded than anyone had seen it in years—at least since the Iceman, George Gervin, had last led the Spurs into playoff contention.

To the fans sitting up near the roof, David Robinson, even stretched to his full height of seven-feet-and-one-inch, looked no bigger than a fingertip. But to every one of the 15,868 in attendance, he was already larger than life. As the revamped Spurs' starting lineup was announced, the crowd began to cheer.

The noise level continued to rise until the announcer shouted out "Number 50, from the United States Naval Academy, playing center," and the thousands roared with one voice.

David slapped five with his teammates, and he took the time to locate his parents in the stands. He had asked them to move to San Antonio to spend his rookie season with him. He bought them a house to live in and set them up with tickets for all the Spurs' home games. And as they had always done when he was at Navy, they sat up in the crowd on this, his Spurs' induction day, ready to cheer him on, shout their advice, and urge him to bear down when his concentration began to flag. But he didn't expect any problems with concentration and focus tonight.

When the national anthem was played, David Robinson stood at attention—stock still, straight and tall. He was ready for duty.

The defending Western conference champion Lakers knew they were facing a different team from the previous year's sorry crew; but until the game began, they didn't know *how different*. Two minutes and two seconds into the contest, they found out. David took a pass inside from Terry Cummings and slammed it home with a powerful reverse dunk. He ruled the boards and dominated the Lakers' centers, former Spur Mychal Thomson and fellow rookie Vlade Divac. With Cummings also overpowering A. C. Green at power forward, the Spurs' inside game was devastating.

Behind the aggressive play of their two big men, San Antonio surged into the lead. But the Lakers were *the* team of the eighties, and they were still fearsome.

Late in the third quarter, with the Spurs ahead 72-61, Los Angeles finally started their move. They scored 9 straight points, cleared the boards, and were speeding downcourt—Laker showtime in action—with Magic ready to take it to the hole. Waiting for him was the rookie.

Mr. Johnson met Mr. Robinson—face-to-face. David raised his hand and diverted Magic's shot from the hoop.

It was David's first, and only, rejection of the evening, and with 1:56 left in the third quarter, it left the Lakers dead. They quickly sank to a double-digit deficit, and the game ended 106-98.

The rookie was unquestionably the star of the game. With his remarkable quickness, David finished with 23 points (most on a succession of dunks and offensive rebounds) and 17 rebounds, including 7 on the offensive glass.

Afterward, the Magic man spoke about the player he saw as a new force in the league. "It's hard to say he's a rookie," remarked Johnson. "He's a man already, you know. Some guys just aren't ever rookies."

☐

When David came into the league, there were a number of fine, productive centers plying their trade in the paint and underneath the boards of the NBA. The great Kareem Abdul-Jabbar was gone from the Lakers, having made his farewell tour the preceding spring. But the wily old pro Robert Parish was still going strong in Boston. Bad Boy Bill Laimbeer was an integral part of the NBA champion Detroit Pistons. And even though he was on the decline, another tough old-timer, Moses Malone of the Atlanta Hawks, could still make his presence felt down in the blocks. But before David arrived in the NBA, two men stood head and shoulders above the crowd.

On December 14th at San Antonio's HemisFair Arena, David Robinson was formally introduced to Hakeem Olajuwon of the Houston Rockets. At the time, Hakeem, along with the Knicks' Patrick Ewing, was generally considered to be one of the two best centers on the planet. An upper-middle-class native of Lagos, Nigeria, Olajuwon was, like David, both an excellent all-around athlete and a latecomer to the game. He had never even picked up a basketball until he was fifteen, when his high school coach recruited the tall soccer and handball star to play in the Nigeria sports festival.

Despite his size and athletic ability, as an American prospect the young African was a complete unknown. When Olajuwon decided to attend college in the United States, he enrolled in the University of Houston because he knew a fellow Nigerian who had played tennis there and because a number of his countrymen were enrolled in nearby Texas Southern University.

When Hakeem called Guy Lewis from the Houston airport, the Cougar coach told him to pay for his own cab ride to the campus. Hakeem, though, refused to be intimidated by American indifference and he worked hard at improving his game. By the end of his undergraduate sojourn, he had twice led his team to the NCAA finals. That summer, he was the NBA's top draft choice. And since his arrival in the league in 1984, he had never averaged below 20 points or 10 rebounds per game.

David, who had always kept his focus better against top-quality opponents, responded to the challenge of playing the strong, mobile, aggressive, and experienced Olajuwon with a brilliant effort. In what Larry Brown believed was David's best game of the season to date, he gave the Houston star no quarter. While Hakeem outrebounded David 16 to 9, and they each had 3 blocks, the rookie's relentless defense forced the Nigerian Rocket to misfire. Olajuwon shot only 5 of 17 from the floor, and was outscored by David 19 to 15 in a 4-point Spur victory.

"You have to give credit where credit is due," said Olajuwon. Robinson "was very aggressive and very, very quick. He's one of the most physical centers I've faced this year. He was really tough."

One month later, on January 13th, David met the league's other great big man, Patrick Ewing, in their first regular season encounter in Madison Square Garden. Like his counterparts in San Antonio and Houston, the New York Knick star came late to the game of basketball. He didn't play until after his thirteenth birthday, when his family moved to Cambridge, Massachusetts, from his native Jamaica. But he learned extraordinarily quickly, and by the time he was a senior at Cambridge Rindge and Latin High School, he was the most highly recruited player in the country. At Georgetown, where he played under John Thompson, he was dominant on both ends of the

floor. And in his four years at the school, he led the
Hoyas to one national championship and two other
near misses in the NCAA finals.

Ewing had come into the league in 1985 with
great expectations, but despite being Rookie of the
Year he had been unable to carry a weak Knick team
into the top ranks of the NBA. It had taken years of
hard work for him to establish himself as Olajuwon's
peer, but by the time the Spurs played the Knicks in
Madison Square Garden in January 1990, Ewing had
proven himself to be one of the league's true super-
stars. Patrick was a remarkably intense and competitive 250-pound strongman with a great shooting
touch and classic post-up moves.

In their first meeting, David outshone Patrick
statistically, but it was to no avail; the Knicks won
the game.

Four nights later, in San Antonio, the two players
met again, and both came prepared to stake out their
territory.

From the first seconds, it was war—mayhem in
the paint. Patrick pounded his way inside, hoping to
cow his lighter opponent into giving ground. But
David would not move an inch. Two minutes into the
contest, Robinson grabbed Ewing from behind and
pulled him to the floor, where they both landed in a
heap. "I was doing what I had to do," said the home-
town favorite. "We were both trying to establish ourselves." The macho play continued throughout the
game, and for forty-six minutes Ewing got the best of
his young adversary. But with the score tied at 90,
Robinson hit the go-ahead basket, a fallaway with
1:27 left.

The Knicks came downcourt, and Patrick, establishing his position down low, put a hip on David. Off balance, Robinson fell back about three and a half feet. Gerald Wilkins, seeing Ewing open momentarily, tried to throw a pass into the post. But he telegraphed it, and in a split second, Number 50, using his remarkable speed, stepped in front of the big Knick to pick off the pass and start a fast break. Knick coach Stu Jackson later recalled how "Robinson was practically on the ground and he got up in a millisecond [to make] the steal. I watched the whole thing and I still can't believe it. . . . I mean, he did what most normal human beings can't do."

But David still wasn't finished. With nineteen seconds to go, Ewing rolled toward the hoop for a dunk. Robinson took off and got his hand on the ball, cleanly rejecting the Knicks' last chance.

In the end, the two centers reversed the roles that they had played in New York four nights earlier. This time Patrick won the battle of the stats—but David won the war. The final score: 101-97, San Antonio.

As he was about to leave the court, Robinson suddenly turned, and with his whole body aching from the confrontation, he came back toward Ewing and slapped him on the back. The two big men shook hands.

David had arrived. He was still the new kid on the block, but there was no question that he belonged in the neighborhood.

□

Twenty-four players were selected to play in the NBA's annual midseason all-star game, but only one was a rookie. As the crowds checked into Miami area hotels for the February 1990 All-Star Weekend, first-year phenom David Robinson was on the cover of the *Miami Herald.* Two weeks earlier the same star had been the subject of the cover story in *Sports Illustrated.*

As part of the pregame hoopla, the *Herald* polled an executive from each of the NBA's 27 teams to get their predictions on which players would dominate the league in the coming decade. To no one's surprise, Michael Jordan was the squad's only unanimous selection. But in the weighted ballot, the top overall vote-getter (who one exec had the temerity to leave off his ballot) was the rookie, David Robinson. The others on the starting five were established young stars Karl Malone, Patrick Ewing, and Kevin Johnson, who edged out the over-30 Magic J sheerly on the basis of age.

Along with the twenty-four basketball players at the pregame All-Star press conference, there were 900 reporters who witnessed the spectacle of Charles Barkley grabbing a microphone out of the hands of a TV reporter and thrusting it in David Robinson's face.

Sir Charles started his interview of King David with the statement: "You have been the impact player of the year. You are one of the best centers in the league right now and you are only a rookie. You are in the same category as Hakeem Olajuwon and Patrick Ewing. If they gave the MVP award right now, you would deserve it."

Of course the ever-loquacious Barkley barely let the embarrassed rookie get a word in edgewise, but he made his point. And he wasn't the only one. Isiah Thomas said, "David's the player of the nineties. He'll probably be the best player in the NBA in another year or two, if he's not already. He'll be the center everybody compares themselves with."

David was not only an All-Star player, for the press in attendance he also proved to be an all-star interview. Except when confronted by big Charles, he was hardly ever at a loss for words. He was charming, congenial, and much in demand among the beat reporters, TV sportscasters, and action photographers in attendance.

About his adjustment to the NBA, Robinson said, "I've already been clotheslined, I've been elbowed in my throat, I've had my eye scratched." He paused. "All this week. That's the league. That's the way it is."

Relishing his role as a newcomer and a student of the game, at one point he pulled a piece of paper out of his pocket and unfolded it. On it was a typewritten reminder from his coach which began: "You must rebound on both ends of the floor."

As the only newcomer in a contest dominated by canny veterans, David needed all the tips he could get. He first had to go up against the Celtics' thirty-six-year-old Robert Parish, whom he had already outplayed in their teams' first meeting. This time, though, Parish changed his game plan, pulling up for jump shots, then faking the rookie off his feet and driving past him for layups. Said Parish: "I guess I still get by because I'm smarter than I used to be."

At times the rookie also played forward, alongside Hakeem Olajuwon. Now he had to line up opposite the league's best defensive player, Detroit's Dennis Rodman, and the Worm turned, bumping and grabbing and stepping in front of Robinson, forcing him into committing errors.

While David had decent stats, his team was never in the game and he rarely had the chance to take off and use his speed in the open court. "What these guys do is humble you," he said. "What I learned today is that I have a lot to learn."

CHAPTER XV

ROOKIE (OF THE) YEAR

Although David Robinson lacked the sophisticated post-up technique of most of basketball's top centers, from the very start of his pro career he was compared to the game's most consistent winner, the great Boston Celtic pivotman of the fifties and sixties, Bill Russell. Speed and quickness had defined the lefthanded Hall of Famer, and observers saw the same factors making the rookie southpaw unique among contemporary big men. And if Robinson didn't have a skyhook like Abdul-Jabbar, or a turnaround like Ewing, neither did Russell, who also scored most of his points on dunks and off the offensive boards. Russell dominated with defense and rebounding, and so, thought virtually everyone who saw him play, could Robinson.

After the Spurs beat his Warriors on December 6th, Golden State coach (and former Russell teammate) Don Nelson proclaimed: "He has everything—strength, quickness, size, speed. He has (all) he's going to need. He's phenomenal."

Another ex-Celtic, Houston Rocket coach Don

Chaney, declared unequivocally, "David has the best
lateral movement and quickness that I've seen since
Russell."

And Warrior Rod Higgins, a small forward often
utilized by Nelson in the post to create matchup
problems for opposing teams, found that his own
quickness was of no help against the rookie. "As
soon as he feels your body on him," said the 6-7
Higgins, "he spins and you can't recover."

No one had ever combined size and speed in one
package the way David did. He had all the tools.

□

The Spurs had planned well for David's arrival. In
Larry Brown, they had hired a coach who was widely
known as a motivator and a teacher. (Brown, of
course, would never have even considered taking the
Spurs' job if the Annapolis graduate hadn't already
been signed up for future delivery.) They also outbid
the Portland Trailblazers to sign sixteen-year veteran
Caldwell Jones, the oldest active player in the NBA.
Jones was not expected to do much on the court (although he did still have the defensive ability to make
opponents miserable for at least a few minutes a
game). His real value to the team was that, as a con-
summate professional and one of the most knowl-
edgeable and articulate men in the business, he could
be an on-the-court coach to young David Robinson.

The Spurs had also put together a group of role-
players who had the talent to compete in the NBA;
David did not have to carry the team by himself. Unlike the Knicks in Ewing's rookie year, or the Rockets
when Olajuwon entered the league, the Spurs could

flat out play, and they could win even when their star center had an off night. "We can do a lot of things. We don't just walk the dog here," declared seven-year veteran Terry Cummings, the 6-9 power forward who had averaged 22 points a game throughout his distinguished career and now willingly shared the work in the trenches with the rookie.

Starting at the point was veteran Maurice Cheeks, who had come over to the Spurs after a decade as the quarterback of the Philadelphia 76ers. A thorough professional, Cheeks had been an integral part of an NBA championship team. He knew how to win, and, having spent most of his career feeding Julius Erving, Charles Barkley, and Moses Malone, he also knew how to take advantage of a star's particular talents.

Joining the two veterans as starters were 22-year-old Willie Anderson and 21-year-old Sean Elliott, both potential all-stars. And the bench—Frank Brickowski, Vernon Maxwell, and David Wingate—gave the squad quality depth. So even though David was the center of attention, the Spurs were not Navy. "I never played with a team with this many good athletes," Cummings said.

With so much talent on the team, and Brown's motion offense and transition game strategy minimizing the need for a classical post-up center, it was easy for David's talents to be showcased and the flaws in his game to be minimized.

The veterans knew what was expected of them, and they understood the team would only go as far as the rookie took them. At the age of thirty-nine, Caldwell "Pops" Jones had forgotten more about the in-

tricacies of post play than his young charge had ever
learned, and he was able and willing to pass on as
much of his experience to the brilliant rookie as
David was ready to take in.

The Spurs' old man marveled at the unique talent
he saw every day in practice. "[Robinson] is so grace-
ful and can get up and down the floor with such ease
that he can control the game in transition," he declared. But Jones, like Coach Brown, understood the
difference between athletic ability and knowledge of
the game. "Potential has killed a lot of people over
the years," he warned, and while he praised Robinson's anticipation, intelligence, and ability to see the
whole picture, he insisted that for him to fulfill his
unlimited potential, David "has got to learn how to
play."

Meanwhile, at the very start of the season Mo
Cheeks recognized that no big man had ever run the
floor like David, and he instinctively understood how
to best take advantage of David's speed. From the
moment he saw the seven-footer outrun most of the
Spurs' guards in practice, he made it clear to his
teammates that "if the big man runs with you [on the
fast break] then you get him the ball."

The carefully assembled combination of solid
veterans, excellent young players, and one superstar
rookie made the Spurs an instant winner. By January
9th, just thirty games into the season, they had already surpassed the previous year's edition of the
Spurs in total victories. Three days later they improved their record to 23 and 8, by beating the Celtics in Boston Garden, ending a winless *decade* on

the fabled parquet floor of the Celts' home court. This team was *for real.*

☐

David's future with the Spurs appeared unlimited; he could take his talent as far as he wanted to. Those who knew him had no doubts about his ability to become one of the best players in the history of the game. There were questions, however, concerning his motivation.

"The game's not in his blood," observed Spurs' assistant coach Gregg Popovich. "One day I showed him something in practice. He said, 'I almost got it. A couple of more months should do it.' He meant a concerto he was composing on his keyboard."

"Sometimes I just find myself watching," David explained, "kind of spacing out, not forcing myself to go down and get in the action."

David still had too much on his mind to concentrate on basketball all the time. "I get a lot of enjoyment out of different things," he said. "Music, people, basketball. But if I'm thinking about my girl, or music, in a game, I drift. If I come into a game focused, I stay focused. Magic [Johnson] was focused for years because basketball was his main interest. Now he's trying to develop other interests. I came into this league with other interests and had to learn to focus on basketball. Life's a learning process. I have to learn to sacrifice things for basketball, but I can't lose my identity. What good is it being the greatest basketball player if you're the most miserable?"

David's fear that a single-minded dedication to

basketball would reduce his enjoyment of life was a constant source of frustration to his coach, Larry Brown. To him, it was plain as day that the Spurs' young center could dominate the league—as long as his head was into it. He had so much intelligence and athletic ability—why couldn't he consistently reach his own highest level? The problem, blurted out the coach, was that "growing up, [Robinson] didn't know if he wanted to be Mozart, Thomas Edison, or Bon Jovi."

"When I talk to David," said Brown, "I talk about Michael, Bird, and Magic. I have so much respect for them because every night, and every day in practice, they lay it on the line. That's why they're the best."

Very few players have the ability to achieve what the great ones accomplish. To do so, the coach explained, requires an uncommon combination of extraordinary natural talent and unshakable resolve.

"David is going to be terrific just like he is," Brown declared. "But if he laid it on the line every night," he concluded, "he might be better than all of them."

David, meanwhile, was still getting by on his blinding speed, lightning reflexes, and tremendous leaping ability. If he ever learned the fine points of post play, Brown knew he would be awesome, absolutely unstoppable.

□

As the season's first half drew to a close, David was dominating, the team was winning, and the Spurs' blend of exuberance and experience had them humming along at a pace that made the league's best franchises stand up and take notice. Nonetheless, the solidity of what the Spurs had accomplished—the irreversibility of their arrival in the top ranks of the NBA—was not completely established until February 21st, less than two weeks after the all-star game, when the Spurs acquired Rod Strickland from the Knicks in exchange for Mo Cheeks.

As the point guard, Cheeks had been instrumental in carrying out Larry Brown's strategies on the court. His ability to keep the offense running smoothly—to get everyone involved while taking advantage of David Robinson's startling speed—was a key component in the team's turnaround. But Maurice was unhappy about the trade that had brought him to the Spurs from Philadelphia. He lived in a hotel, did his job, but was clearly homesick for the East Coast. Sensing that the 33-year-old Cheeks might retire rather than continue to play in Texas, General Manager Bob Bass decided to unload him while he was still marketable.

Fortunately for the Spurs, Strickland was caught in an uncomfortable situation of his own in New York. The Knicks were unable to decide which of their two young point guards—Rod or Mark Jackson —they wanted as the starter, and as a result the play of both men suffered. Finally, the disgruntled Strickland was sent to San Antonio, where he was handed the starting job.

The question was could the Spurs continue to win with the volatile but talented Rod Strickland replacing the cool, experienced head of Mo Cheeks? Or had they bartered their present for an uncertain future?

The answers came immediately, when, in Strickland's first game in San Antonio, he stepped in and handed out 9 assists in a 10-point victory over Minnesota.

The Spurs were building their present with what was looking more and more like the NBA's team of the future. With Cummings as the only veteran starter (the other four were all either rookies or second-year players), their starting unit was the youngest in the league, with an average age of just twenty-four years.

□

Despite their youth and lack of experience, the team continued to win. But a short cold spell, starting with an 18-point loss in Houston on March 26th, dropped them to second place in the Midwest Division behind Utah by early April. On April 8th, even though David rose to the occasion with a brilliant 36-point, 19-rebound performance, they lost to the Trailblazers in Portland and appeared to be falling out of the race for the division title. They were 49 and 26, and had only seven games left to catch first-place Utah.

After winning their next four in a row, they were still behind—but closing fast and still in the fight. Then, on April 18th, they faced the Jazz at home in front of a packed house.

For days, David could think of nothing but the upcoming confrontation in the HemisFair Arena. "And," he said, "I *never* think about games ahead of time." He came out more focused than he'd ever been in the pros. On offense, he was a blur, shooting by Utah's huge 7-4, 290-pound center, Mark Eaton, time and again for rim-rattling dunks. Finally, as David started spinning away for yet another easy hoop, the frustrated Eaton grabbed him by the jersey and yanked him away from the basket. But it didn't help; David still shot 14 for 18 from the floor.

On the other end of the court the sensational Mr. Robinson was just as intense and every bit as effective. He had never been so quick, jumping out to contest every shot (he blocked five), and challenge every pass into the paint. And he wasn't just roaming the middle, guarding the relatively immobile defensive specialist Eaton—it was his job to stop Karl Malone one on one. Late in the game, the rookie leaned, pushed, muscled, and totally frustrated the Mailman until finally the best power forward in the game lost his cool—and got himself whistled for an offensive foul. Robinson's brilliant defensive effort forced Malone into an uncharacteristic 6 for 19 from the floor. With David also dominating both boards, San Antonio won easily—and sailed home to take the division title.

□

As the playoffs began, Portland Coach Rick Adelman echoed what Magic had said six months earlier, at the start of the regular season. Robinson, he declared, was "as much a rookie center as Magic Johnson was a rookie guard in his first year." And Adelman, whose Trailblazers were expected to face the Spurs in the second round of the playoffs, surely remembered how Magic had ended that season—leading his team to an NBA title.

At about the same time, David was asked which of the league's centers gave him the most trouble. He praised Olajuwon, Ewing, Parish, and Malone, but admitted that the Trailblazer front line was the most difficult for him to handle. With the Blazers, the problem wasn't a single dominating player. "They've got all those big bodies," he said, "and they make you work for everything. You spend the whole game bouncing off people."

Both the Spurs and the Blazers easily swept their first-round series, setting up a Western Conference semifinal between two of the hottest teams in the league.

It was a classic series, and it went to the limit.

Going in, the Spurs had won ten games in a row, but the Blazers, with a regular season record of 59 and 23, held the homecourt advantage. And Portland, with a 35-6 regular season record at the cozy Memorial Coliseum, was virtually unbeatable at home.

In game one, playing in front of their usual rabid sellout crowd, they were confident and aggressive. The Spurs, meanwhile, came out flat and allowed themselves to be dominated underneath. The big Blazer frontcourt, led by old pro Buck Williams, controlled the boards, breezing by Robinson and Cummings for layups and rebounds. While San Antonio was out of sync, Portland's aggressive defense pushed David off the block. They bumped and shoved and double teamed the ball down low, frustrating the Spurs' two big men and forcing San Antonio to rely

on their perimeter game. As a result, when the two
squads arrived in Texas, the home team was two
games in the hole.

The Spurs had their backs to the wall. Things
hadn't looked so dark in the old city since 1836,
when General Santa Anna's troops surrounded and
laid siege to the Alamo. David knew something was
wrong with the way he had played in Portland, but he
couldn't put his finger on what it was. Finally, he
watched tapes of the games and *analyzed* the problem—he wasn't putting his body on the Blazers on
the defensive end, and by not making contact, he was
letting the Portland centers slide by him unnoticed to
get inside position under the boards.

In game three David concentrated on correcting
the problem. He stepped up his defense, dominating
inside with eight blocks and innumerable intimida-
tions. His heroics helped set up the Spurs' transition
game, which worked to perfection. With Rod Strickland running the show and distributing the ball beau-
tifully (he finished with 17 assists) and David time
and again outrunning his slower opponents
downcourt for emphatic, get-out-of-my-way-I'm-
coming-through slam dunks, it was a blowout,
121-98.

At the start of game four, the Trailblazers could
do no wrong. They scored virtually every time they
came down the floor until late in the first quarter,
when David came alive with an electrifying series of
defensive plays. As Buck Williams aggressively took
the ball to the hole, David came from behind and
exploded off the floor—just in time to flick the shot
away. On the Blazers' next trip downcourt, the

Spurs' center reached out to snare a crosscourt pass
and fire the ball ahead for a quick transition basket.
Seconds later, Portland challenged the Spurs' big
man again, and he once again got his hand on the ball
for a rejection.

In less than a minute Number 50 had wreaked
havoc on the Blazer offense, and by forcing Portland
into a constant awareness of his presence, like a big
cat poised to strike without warning, he had transformed the entire complexion of the game. Although
the score was still 24-17 Blazers, Portland was obviously deflated, the arena was going wild with anticipation—and the Spurs were still alive.

While David dominated on defense, Cummings
took control on offense, calling for the ball, pounding
it inside, crashing the boards and pulling up for
jumpers. Gradually—inexorably—the Spurs took
control, and by the end they had another easy victory,
115-105.

After the game, a radio interviewer offhandedly
remarked to Larry Brown that it was a rough game
for the Admiral. "What do you mean?" asked the
astonished coach. His star had finished with 21
points, 10 boards, and 4 blocked shots. Besides,
Brown pointed out, Robinson clogged the middle,
shot 50 percent from the floor (even though he was
double-teamed most of the game), and his team won.

But game five, back on Portland's home court,
was a heartbreaking, double overtime 138-132 loss
for the Spurs. If they had managed to win, they
would have gone back to San Antonio with a chance
to close out the series on their home court, but they
couldn't quite pull it off. Instead, when they took the

floor in Texas for game six, the Spurs' task was just to keep their hopes alive. And though they came away with another easy victory, their reward was a return trip into enemy territory for one last decisive battle.

On the evening of May 19th, the two teams reconvened in Portland. Kevin Duckworth, the massive Trailblazer center who had been out with an injury, was back in the starting lineup, reuniting the league's top rebounding front court. Early in the first quarter, Robinson asserted himself with a hard block, but before the period ended, the Blazers caught fire, going on an 18-4 run to lead 31-24. Robinson, meanwhile, disappeared; he once again seemed to be lost in an alternate universe. With no offense coming out of the low post, the Spurs became increasingly nettled; only the clutch shooting of Anderson and Cummings kept them in the game. The tension mounted, until late in the first half when Rod Strickland vented his frustration by throwing a forearm to the face of Portland's Yugoslavian sharpshooter, Drazen Petrovic. A moment later Robinson went over the top for a rebound, and was whistled for his third foul; Brown pulled him out for the rest of the half.

At the start of the second half, although David continued his disappearing act on offense, he became a human vacuum cleaner off the defensive boards, and as a result San Antonio was able to push the ball up the floor for easy transition baskets. Suddenly, with 3:20 left in the third quarter, the Portland lead was down to 2—and David, despite snaring 11 rebounds, had scored an almost inconceivable 4 points all night.

In the fourth quarter, to the disbelief of the Port-

land home crowd, Robinson began to quietly dominate—and the Spurs surged into the lead. David asserted himself; he called for the ball, hit a
turnaround, sped downcourt to finish a fast break,
and ended up with 7 points and 6 rebounds in the
period. On defense, meanwhile, he owned the lane,
and with his lanky arms and legs extending in all
directions like a giant octopus, he prevented any pen-
etration into his territory.

With two minutes left, the score stood at 97-90
San Antonio, and it looked certain that the Spurs
would pull off a major upset and make it to the Western final against the Lakers. But Portland stormed
back to deadlock the count at the end of regulation.

In the overtime, while the Trailblazers continued
to show their experience, the young Spurs—led by
their rookie center—refused to fold. With the score
103-101 Portland, David was double-teamed in the
post. A couple of quick fakes and he was free, fifteen
feet from the hoop. With the ball in his hands, he hit
a turnaround jumper—103-103.

But on this night, the Admiral's ship just
wouldn't come in. After Portland regained the lead,
Rocket Rod Strickland penetrated, and under heavy
pressure, wildly threw the ball over his head—to no
one. After the crucial turnover, Strickland raced
downcourt to stop the Trailblazer fast break, but was
called for a deliberate foul.

Heartbreak hotel.

The young Spurs couldn't quite overcome the
Blazers' experience and home court advantage. They
took the eventual Western Conference champs to the

limit twice, but they came up short. For San Antonio, that championship season would have to wait.

□

Despite the disappointing loss to Portland, David and his teammates were able to look back at the season with pride. In one short year, they had come so far, from a doormat to a contender.

By the end of the regular season, David had led the Spurs to the greatest single turnaround in league history. San Antonio finished with 56 wins and only 26 losses, a 35-game improvement over the previous year's 21-61 record. The Spurs' revival outshone even the Celtics' 32-game improvement in Larry Bird's rookie year and the Milwaukee Bucks' 29-game swing in Kareem Abdul-Jabbar's first season.

The Spurs finished with a winning record in every month of the regular season, lost no more than three straight at any time, and capped off the campaign with a seven-game winning streak. They also drew a franchise record 603,660 fans to their forty-one home games, for an average of 14,723 per game.

There was no question that despite all the key contributions of San Antonio's other fine players, one man stood above the rest. David was only the second player in NBA history to win Rookie of the Month honors in every one of the six months of the regular season. For his play in the final week, when the Spurs completed the stretch drive that brought them their division title, he was voted the league's Player of the Week. He finished ninth in the league in scoring (averaging 24.3 points per game), second in rebounding (12 per game), third in blocked shots

(3.89), twentieth in steals (1.68), and his .531 shooting percentage placed him fifteenth in the league in
that category. He was the unanimous choice of the
ninety-two sports writers and broadcasters who
voted for Rookie of the Year, and was, along with
Magic Johnson, Michael Jordan, Patrick Ewing,
Charles Barkley, Karl Malone, and Hakeem
Olajuwon, a top candidate for the league's Most Valuable Player. (In the computer-generated TENDEX
ratings, a comparison of each of the league's players
computed by combining stats in ten different categories, he tied Karl Malone for second in the league
behind Michael Jordan.) By any measure, David was
already one of the league's top performers.

"In one season," Larry Brown remarked, "this
has become David's team. He is its heart and soul.
I'm not sure he realizes that yet, because everything
has happened so quickly. But the more he grows into
that role, the better he'll become and the better the
team will become."

CHAPTER XVI

SOPHOMORE SLUMP

Going into David's second season, the Spurs felt optimistic about their chances of winning the NBA championship. They were still younger than any of the other contenders, but they had gone through a trial by fire the previous year and come within a whisker of beating the eventual Western conference champs. With a year of experience under their belts, they felt they could only get better.

Both Terry Cummings and Willie Anderson had received summertime votes of confidence from management, with each signing a lucrative four-year contract extension.

Management had also made some changes which seemed to improve the depth and versatility of the squad. They brought veteran swing man Paul Pressey over from the Milwaukee Bucks in exchange for Frank Brickowski, thereby adding a cool consistent head to the backcourt. They also brought another big banger into the mix by obtaining veteran power forward Sidney Green from Orlando to spell Terry Cummings (and occasionally David). And David Greenwood came back from Detroit, where he had been a little-used substitute on a championship team, plus they signed three promising rookies.

As for the 25-year-old anchor of the team, it was almost unthinkable that he wouldn't improve. Each year since he started playing basketball as a high school senior back in Virginia he had taken his game up another notch. And as the season approached, he said, "I'm getting a better feel on how to focus. I know I have to be up for every game and maintain my intensity. I kind of woke up during the playoffs against the Blazers. I'll improve in that area this year."

He also said he would be more of a vocal team leader, pushing his teammates to put out maximum effort. And as for the Spurs, he said, "Our goals will be a division title, conference title, and then league title."

They all seemed like reasonable expectations with Admiral Robinson at the helm.

□

But by the end of the exhibition schedule, things started to sour. Just before opening night, Willie Anderson was placed on injured reserve with stress fractures in his shins. Rod Strickland was also out with an injury, and the 1990–91 Spurs made their official debut with understudies at both guard spots.

Even without their young backcourt, though, the Spurs were a team to be watched. Unlike the previous year, when NBC all but ignored them, this time the network put their November 3rd season opener on national television. Matched up against Magic

Johnson and the Lakers at the HemisFair Arena, Terry (T.C.) Cummings and Paul Pressey led the Spurs from a shaky start and a 14-point first quarter deficit to win going away, 110-99.

Within two weeks, both Strickland and Anderson returned to the lineup, but somehow, despite winning far more often than they lost, the Spurs seemed curiously out of sync. The roster had certainly improved on paper, but the game was played on the court, and the team concept that had guided them the previous year now appeared to be on the back burner. On November 25th, the red-hot Blazers burned the Spurs with a 49-18 first period; two games later, in L.A., they were again thoroughly outplayed, this time by the Lakers. But it wasn't just the good teams they had problems with; they lost to the Warriors, barely beat the mediocre Dallas Mavericks, and weren't even able to blow out the woeful Denver Nuggets.

The Spurs also continued to fall victim to injuries. Sidney Green left the bench for most of December with bone spurs, Paul Pressey came up hobbled and missed a few games, and rookie Sean Higgins was also injured. On December 11th, Terry Cummings suffered a hyperextended knee. Among the starters, only David and Sean Elliott were able to go out on the court each night.

However, despite all the team's problems, David was still simply looking like the best basketball player in the universe.

On December 18th, Hakeem Olajuwon told *USA Today* that his counterpart on the Spurs would have "to pay his dues before he's on the level with Patrick and myself." But that same night, David blocked 4 of Hakeem's shots, grabbed 13 rebounds and carried his team to a one-point comeback victory over the Rockets in Houston. (Olajuwon soon accepted Robinson's application for membership in the exclusive supercenters club, telling a *Sporting News* correspondent, "He's one of us now.")

David, meanwhile, continued on his roll. In a two-week period between December 28th and January 12th he finished with three triple-doubles. And more often than not, he led the Spurs in scoring, rebounding, and blocks.

David carried the shaky team on his back. San Antonio had an injury list that seemed to grow longer by the day, and they showed a disturbing lack of oncourt harmony. Yet largely through Robinson's efforts they continued to win. By the time they blew out division rival Utah by 20 points on the twelfth of January (David: 22 points, 18 rebounds, 11 blocked shots), the Spurs were 24-8. They had the third best record in the league, despite playing 18 of their first 32 games on the road. They had already missed well over 40 player games because of injury, compared to the previous season's *total* of 15. The rest of the league wondered what they would do if they ever got healthy and started playing together.

□

Throughout the season, David stood straighter and taller than ever when "The Star-Spangled Banner" was played. Each time he heard the strains of the national anthem he couldn't help but think of his peers who were on the sea and in the desert half a world away.

Operation Desert Shield had been launched way back in August, when the first American troops were dispatched to Saudi Arabia in response to Iraqi dictator Saddam Hussein's invasion of neighboring Kuwait. Right after the start of the regular season, President Bush announced his intention to double the size of the U.S. presence in the area, and tens of thousands of armed forces personnel began streaming into the Middle East each week.

As the two sides grew closer to war, the concerned Naval reservist paused to reflect on the circumstances that led him to the NBA while his Annapolis classmates were being rushed to the flashpoint in the Persian Gulf. "It's a very real possibility I would be in the Mideast if I hadn't grown," he said. "I think about those guys every day."

Even at the beginning, he had feared for their safety and imagined himself in their shoes, waiting to receive the orders to fight. He tried not to let the talk of war affect his play, but he was concerned, and deeply hoped that conflict could be avoided. He knew from his own training that while he was engaged in fun and games, the guys over there were involved in life and death. He spoke frequently with Gregg Popovich, who as a 1970 Air Force Academy graduate had also served in the armed forces, and the two men shared their feelings about what was happening overseas.

Meanwhile the United Nations Security Council, tiring of Saddam Hussein's intransigence and refusal to abandon the armed annexation of his neighbor, set a deadline of midnight January 15th for Iraq to begin its withdrawal. If Saddam did not accept the U.N. resolutions by that date, President Bush warned, Iraq would face destruction.

During the first weeks of 1991, David and some of his teammates gathered around the locker room TV before virtually every game to watch the news. Willie Anderson's brother was stationed in the Gulf. So were an ever-increasing number of David's friends.

On January 15th, *The National* sports daily reported that if war broke out, David Robinson's chances of being called to active duty—despite his height—were "pretty good." An unnamed officer at the San Antonio Naval Reserve Center told the paper, "I'm certain his chances would increase a great deal." Although an official Navy spokeswoman said that the chances of calling anyone of Lieutenant Robinson's status was pretty remote, David said, "If I have to serve, I'll serve and go eagerly. I don't consider myself different than anybody else."

The same night, playing against the Jazz in Salt Lake City, San Antonio's big man left Mark Eaton in his tracks three times in the first nine minutes and the Spurs raced to a 9-point lead. But when David left for a short breather, the Jazz immediately went on an 11-2 tear to tie the score. Things went from bad to worse for the undermanned Spurs (who were missing Terry Cummings), and despite a few more personal highlights for David, the game soon got out of hand. By the end it was a total wipeout, a 22-point loss for the Spurs to their closest competitors in the division.

When the buzzer sounded to end the game it was

9:41 P.M., mountain time, just nineteen minutes before midnight in Washington. As David and his teammates returned to the visitors' locker room, the clock was ticking toward high noon for Saddam Hussein and George Bush.

The press was all over David, asking for a comment from the Navy man about the imminent outbreak of war. All of a sudden the game with the Jazz was a thousand miles away. "I think the major concern is whether we have a war or not," he said quietly. "I'm hoping that something can be done, because there's a lot of people who are going to die who just don't need to die."

As the force of history swept across his consciousness, bouncing a basketball, slamming it through a hoop, running down a hardwood court, and jumping higher and faster and truer than the other guy—even being the best—suddenly became very insignificant. It became a struggle for David to remain focused. His head and his heart simply weren't into the game. They were halfway around the world.

The next night in Dallas and for weeks thereafter, David was, like millions of other Americans, transfixed by the events unfolding in the Persian Gulf. He watched the bombing of Baghdad on CNN with his teammates and coaches until it was time to take the court. Then he tried to put it out of his mind.

"At first, I was like most people—I would just sit, wait, and watch," David said. "I got hammered for three or four games," he later recalled. "I was awful."

But in fact, the slump that he, his coaches, and

the press attributed to his feelings about the war largely did not show up in the statistics. In the first five games after the air war began, David led the Spurs to four victories and averaged over 28 points and almost 15 rebounds a game.

Other events, however, did affect both his and the team's play.

□

On January 28th, in a game against Seattle, Terry Cummings broke his hand. Less than a week later, in the wee hours of February 2nd, Rod Strickland got into a fight in the parking lot of a San Antonio night-club called "Illusions" and broke his hand. Suddenly the Spurs' title hopes looked like pure fantasy.

When Strickland's hand was placed in a cast, the Spurs' record was 31 and 11. They were two games ahead of the previous year's pace, and three up on Utah in the race for the Midwest Division title. But now they had neither T.C. banging the boards nor Rocket Rod pushing the ball upcourt on the break. With David still in a minor funk, the losses were too much to overcome.

With Cummings out of the lineup, Larry Brown reluctantly moved David to power forward and started rookie Dwayne Schintzius at center. With Strickland out, the team became more methodical. They stopped pushing the ball upcourt and became much more of a halfcourt-style team. With the transition game cut off, David's speed, particularly his effectiveness in filling the lanes on the fast break, was negated.

For the first time since David's arrival in San Antonio, the Spurs began to lose.

Yet despite the sinking state of the team, David's star continued to rise. By general consensus, he was now considered the premier center (and one of the top draws) in the league. He was cheered wildly in rival arenas throughout the NBA, and had become, with his brilliant play and military background, an irresistible focus of attention. As he wrestled with his feelings about the war, tried to make sense of the role God had put him in, and attempted to do everything for his slumping and shorthanded team, Davidmania became—almost by the moment—more intense and overwhelming.

One night, while he sat in the Dallas Airport, studying a book called *The Craft of Lyric Writing* (he and T.C. were collaborating on some new songs), a young woman—a stranger—handed him her baby and asked if she could take a photo of the two together. At the airport in Salt Lake City, the Creighton women's basketball team spotted him, and he agreed to pose with them for a group shot. Everywhere he went, he was mobbed, with people standing in line for his autograph.

To relax—to get away from the pressure of performing, of public appearances, and of the war—David would pick up the alto sax he'd begun carrying with him a few months earlier, and struggle through a tune; or he'd sit at the piano to chord out a passable rendition of a contemporary jazz piece, or he'd try to fit new lyrics in with a melody. But there was so little time, and no place except behind a locked door, to be by himself.

□

On February 9th when David joined the 1991 All-Star squad in Charlotte as the Western Conference's top vote-getter, he was the league's leading rebounder (with 13.2 rebounds per game), the top shot-blocker (4.24), and he was sixth in the league in scoring (with a 26.3 points per game average).

But in the game itself, his old problem—foul trouble—plagued him again. Still, in just 18 minutes of action, he scored 16 points, grabbed 6 rebounds, drew some gasps with his dunks, blocked three shots (including a Jordan layup), and engaged in his usual ferocious battle in the trenches with Ewing (he stole an alley-oop pass intended for the Knick center). "He's a great player," said Charles Barkley with his tongue firmly in his cheek, "but he should quit hacking."

After All-Star Weekend, David returned to San Antonio to rejoin his struggling team. By the time Terry came back on the 22nd, the Spurs had lost three in a row and their record had dropped to 33 and 16. When the Persian Gulf war ended on February 27th, six weeks after it began, San Antonio was no longer in first place.

The next night, the Spurs jumped out to a 19-1 lead over the Knicks in Madison Square Garden. But then Patrick Ewing caught fire. The inspired New York center dunked and hit turnarounds as a helpless David watched him bring the Knicks back. The New Yorkers won 100-93, completing the Spurs' first losing month in David's two pro seasons.

The month-long absence of Rod and Terry had

put a spotlight on David's biggest weakness, his lack
of a strong post-up game. "The team was looking for
me to score at the end of the game," he said. "That
was a time when I did need a go-to move and I didn't
have it, so it made it kind of tough. I definitely think
it would be a big, big advantage if I had one."

By the time Strickland came off the injured list
on March 19th, the Spurs were 41 and 22. At last,
the team was intact, and it looked like things might
finally come together for them. But the injuries to
Rod and Terry had taken their toll. Where before
there was apparent harmony, now there was friction
between Cummings and Coach Brown, who questioned T.C.'s intensity and shot selection.

And Rod's hand still hurt. Sometimes, even a
month after he was back in action, it was unbearable.
The Spurs' best ball handler had to dribble and pass
with a splint on his right hand: even though he could
still run, he couldn't push the ball upcourt the way he
did before the injury, and he didn't have nearly the
control. After being back in the lineup three weeks,
Rod said, "I usually average about 2.5 turnovers.
Now I'm at 5.5 to 6." And although the Spurs did
play better (winning 13 of their last 17 games), they
never got completely back into sync.

"I figured we'd be more stable this year," said
David as the team fought Utah for the Midwest Division title. "The thing we're lacking is cohesiveness
and confidence. We should be a lot better team this
year, but I don't think we are."

In the next to the last game of the regular season,
the Spurs went into Denver's McNichols Arena to
play the league's worst team, the horrifyingly inept

Nuggets. Denver had lost ten straight, and the Spurs breezed into the final quarter with an 11-point lead. They had no business losing. Yet, despite David's 27 points, 13 rebounds, and 7 blocks, they gave the game away, coming out on the short end of a 125-122 count.

The normally calm, cool, and collected Mr. Robinson was in a rage. Boarding the team bus, he began to shout at his teammates that they didn't deserve to be Midwest Division champions. "I can't remember when I've been more angry," he said. "I was really mad."

But David's anger, and the sting of losing to the league's worst team, motivated the entire squad to play hard and together. Two days later, in their regular season finale against Dallas, the Spurs raced out to a 35-16 margin at the end of the first quarter and they never looked back.

□

The Spurs went into the playoffs against Golden State confident that they had regained their touch. "I'm excited," said Robinson. "I know we're not going to be giving away any games like we did the other night [against Denver]."

But this time the damage was done by Warrior coach Don Nelson, who set the terms of the confrontation by going to a long-range bombing, four-guard lineup. The move created insurmountable matchup problems for the Spurs.

After San Antonio won the first game behind a combined 98 points from David, Willie Anderson, and Rod Strickland, the small, quick Warriors attacked. They double- and triple-teamed the San Antonio center, daring the Spurs to hit from outside. And even though David gave the Midwest Conference champions a significant advantage off the boards, they couldn't run against Golden State.

"They outplayed us," said a frustrated Terry Cummings after the Warriors' big three, (plus Sarunas Marciulionis) all scored over 20 points to help them take a two-one lead in the series. "We allowed them to dictate the flow of each of the last two games. We have to play our game and not get into the up and down game they like."

But San Antonio's style was also a running game, and they simply couldn't keep up with the Warriors, losing game four and the series 110-97.

David shot nearly 70 percent from the floor and averaged over 25 points a game in the playoffs against the Warriors, but he was no match for Golden State's sharpshooting trio, Tim Hardaway, Chris Mullin, and Mitch Richmond, each of whom averaged well over 20 points a game.

It was a bitter defeat. And unlike the previous year's playoff loss to the Blazers (which could be interpreted as a learning experience), this time no one felt good.

□

Despite the rash of serious injuries, the Spurs' regular season record was only one game worse than the previous year. The disappointing loss in the playoffs was largely a result of the brilliant strategy formulated by Warrior coach Don Nelson, but it also came about because of San Antonio's complete lack of an outside shooting threat (they hit only 3 for 26 as a team from three-point range during the playoffs, compared to Golden State's 20 for 52).

After the loss to the Warriors, there was suddenly a lot of talk about breaking up the Spurs. Only a few months earlier, management and the press had been calling them the championship team of the future; now, however, there were strong indications that three of the five starters were expendable, with only Sean Elliott and David considered untouchable.

David Robinson finished third in the league's MVP balloting, behind Michael Jordan and Magic Johnson. His personal statistics were even better than in his rookie year, and he was the only player in the league to finish in the top ten in four statistical categories (rebounding, scoring, blocked shots, and field goal percentage). But he wasn't happy.

"There's no doubt we didn't have the chemistry on the floor this year that we did last year," he said. "We were much deeper this year, more confident in individual players, and we didn't even accomplish the same thing."

David did, however, understand that "it's a matter of learning what it takes to win. I think those are some of the changes that we're going through right now. When you play all year you've got to realize that the playoffs are the only time that *really* matters."

Personal glory was nice, but for David it was no substitute for winning.

CHAPTER XVII

MARKETING MR. ROBINSON

Fame.

As a kid growing up in Virginia he never expected it. As an All-American candidate at Annapolis he never counted on it. But by the time he walked off with College Player of the Year honors in 1987 he had it.

To the media, the public and, the marketing experts who match product with personality, David was the complete package. He was a hot property.

Perhaps, a lifetime ago, way back when he was still at the Naval Academy, he was aware of how fame would change his life (and be coupled irrevocably and incredibly with fortune). Back then, it was his shining smile that had caught the eye of the American Association of Orthodontists, who asked the Navy if he could become their official spokesperson (the brass said no) and who put him on the cover of their patient newsletter under the headline "Basketball Star Lights Up Courts with Smile."

But perhaps David wasn't cognizant of how marketable a seven-foot-one-inch Naval officer, classical
pianist, computer nerd, articulate and earnest
straight-arrow—and, of course, world-class athlete—
could be until he graduated from Annapolis.

Because at that very moment the representatives
of corporate America descended on him like a horde
of prospectors in the Sierra foothills, panning for
gold in the David Robinson mother lode. Savvy ad
execs and marketing directors knew, long before he
traded in his Navy blues to bounce a round ball in
Spurs' silver and black—even when he was stuck in
King's Bay, poring over submarine dock construction
specs for the Navy—that the handsome young Navy
man projected an image that they wanted to sell. And
the public wanted to buy.

While he was still in the service, the Navy had
also caught on to what it had in Ensign Robinson.
The brass realized that keeping him under wraps in
an isolated base was not going to help them bring
new crewmen onboard, and after a few months of
enforced anonymity they put him to work earning his
eighteen-thousand-dollar-a-year salary as a slam-
dunking ace recruiter for the Navy.

While training for the Olympics, David spoke on
behalf of the Naval District of Washington Recruiting
Command at D.C. area high schools in the spring of
1988. He appeared for engagements in his dress
blues, his shiny black shoes, and with a gold and blue
button that ordered young people to "Say No to
Drugs, Say Yes to the Navy."

David was a living, breathing, walking, talking
recruiting poster, and he was also always able to

charm the brass—in the line of duty. He played golf
with admirals, posed for pictures with their wives,
and shook hands at every event his superiors deemed
appropriate.

"The Navy owns me," David said. "They get to
use me any way they want. . . . When they want me
to go speak at the Navy Ball, it's not like I have a
choice. I say, 'Yes, sir, I've always wanted to speak at
the Navy Ball, sir.' "

But while the Navy was getting a free ride in pro-
moting and marketing the world's tallest junior officer, David was also being shopped by his agent, Lee
Fentress. Fentress was commanding hefty fares from
the many companies who wanted to promote their
products with the image of a tall black basketball-
playing Renaissance man.

It turned out that David was perfect for Franklin
Sports, Inc., a Massachusetts-based family-owned
sporting goods company that had superstar personal-
ities Don Mattingly, Wade Boggs, and Mike Schmidt
under exclusive contract for its extensive baseball
product line, as well as Herschel Walker and Sugar
Ray Leonard, respectively, as its signature stars on
football and boxing merchandise. In the summer of
1987, Franklin was preparing to release a new line of
basketball-related merchandise to coincide with the
1988 Olympics, and the company needed a great
player who was also, as their representative John Bal-
las said, "an All-American guy." In David they found
the perfect pitchman—a future pro powerhouse who
was also expected to be the star of the U.S. Olympic
team. Even before David signed with the Spurs, Fentress and Franklin negotiated a five-year agreement,

estimated at the time to be worth a potential million dollars a year.

□

Once David signed the sporting goods contract, Nike, Reebok, and Converse started looking at the big man's feet.

At first it appeared that Reebok had the inside track. The company was a latecomer to the idea of signing high-profile athlete-endorsers to promote their products, but Michael Jordan's high-flying success at Nike led them to rethink their strategy. To outsiders, David and Reebok seemed like a perfect fit.

Converse was the official sneaker of the U.S. Olympic team, and their ads starred Magic and Bird. Despite already having two of the game's top players pitching their high tops, they were very interested in the young Navy man. "We look for the best player on teams, but more important, we look for people who can transcend basketball—be a spokesman for the company off the court," said Gary Stokan, national basketball manager for Converse. "David Robinson is *that* kind of person."

Nike had already soared into its own marketing universe with Michael and the Air Jordan line. The company's director of promotions Fred Schreyer said he didn't think anyone else was in Jordan's class, but he was intrigued by David, thinking the young Navy man "could transcend the traditional barriers because of his [educational] background." But whether it was just a negotiating strategy or a true statement of his point of view, the Nike executive also declared,

"Centers just don't sell shoes. Ten- to eighteen-year-olds identify with smaller or quicker players like Magic or Jordan, not with Kareem, Ewing, or Robinson."

David and Lee Fentress moved quickly, setting up meetings with representatives of all three companies within months of his graduation from the Academy. In the end, despite some negative public signals, it was Nike that came out on the other side of the dotted line. Well before David signed with the Spurs, he executed a million-dollar, five-year deal with the Beaverton, Oregon, company.

To further increase Robinson's marquee value during his active duty years, the ensign also signed a contract to do an instructional series for ABC-TV's college basketball halftime shows; he wrote occasional "diaries" for *The Washington Post* during the Pan Am Games and again during the Olympics; and he even considered writing an autobiographical book focusing on his life at the Naval Academy.

Despite the extraordinary whirlwind of commercial activity, it was necessary for David to maintain his "amateur" status during his time on active duty, in order to play in the Pan Am Games and the Olympics. With the approval of amateur athletic officials, all of the emerging star's income (other than his Navy salary) was thus deposited into the David Robinson Trust Fund, with Advantage International serving as the trustee and David allowed to draw upon the account for expenses.

While David relied in large measure on Lee Fentress's marketing and financial acumen, the self-reliant young officer also wanted to maintain some direct

control on how his business affairs were conducted.
In order to separate the commercial tasks which were
clearly Advantage's (such as negotiating major product endorsement deals), from those that would be
better taken care of in a more low-key and personal
manner, David formed The Robinson Group in April
of 1988, with his father as president, his mother as
executive vice president, and his cousin Aldrich
Mitchell as senior vice president.

The group was incorporated to handle all of
David's day-to-day promotions, to take care of his
voluminous correspondence and to sift through the
numerous requests for his time, services, and money.

In the summer of 1989, when David was released from active duty and moved to San Antonio to
join the Spurs, The Robinson Group became the um-
brella organization that handled all his local activities. The company set up shop in Texas with David's
mother taking care of his mail and scheduling, his
father in charge of marketing and day-to-day operations, and Aldrich (a graduate of Stanford in eco-
nomics and a former international banker) as David's
chief investment adviser. The executives meet several
times a week, with the family advising and David—as
the CEO—making final decisions.

□

By the middle of David's rookie year, he had become
larger than life. While some stars, like Michael and
Magic, seemed totally comfortable in the fishbowl of
fame, it was more of a mixed blessing for David. He
felt he had a responsibility, as a celebrity, to be a role
model. He tried to be courteous and gracious all the

time. But he also felt the constraints on his time and on his ability to just be himself.

"You don't know what a Michael Jordan has to deal with until you see it," he said at the All-Star break in February 1990. "Now I see it. You want to be the same person all the time to everyone. But I'm not in a good mood all the time. And when someone is rude or pushy, or when the fans bum rush you . . . well, it's hard. But I'm lucky, because I usually don't let things bother me."

He tried always to remain the unflappable Mr. Robinson.

David was deeply concerned about the image he projected. He consistently wanted the public to view him as not just another superjock in it only for the money. David had always seen himself as a serious person (with a sense of humor), as a well-rounded personality, as a Renaissance man equally comfortable converting a spare at a bowling alley or playing a Beethoven sonata on a grand piano, a man who excels in a variety of academic disciplines, stands at attention to "The Star-Spangled Banner," and serves as a model of moral rectitude. Perhaps the most interesting aspect of the David Robinson image is that the persona accurately reflects the man himself.

From the time he started making product endorsements, he looked to companies that were reputable and willing to give something back to the community, that would, he said, "help me get my message across about the positive things in life."

And because of David's feelings about the responsibility of the privileged to help the disadvantaged, Nike, Franklin Sports, and Casio (his third

major national sponsor) have all donated products to
local community-support organizations with which
he is involved. David himself buys fifty tickets in the
HemisFair Arena's Upper Deck (an area now known
as Mr. Robinson's Neighborhood) for each Spurs'
home game which he distributes to kids "selected by
teachers across the city for their academic achievement."

He also actively supports Youth Alternatives
Inc., Boys and Girls Clubs of San Antonio, and the I
Have a Dream Foundation with both time and
money.

He has been involved with the I Have A Dream
Foundation since it first began working in the San
Antonio area. In the beginning, he appeared at benefits and was the focus of a poster that read, "Yes,
David, I can see the dream. . . ." He told elementary
school kids that "It's cool to be intelligent." And in
January 1991 he put his money where his mouth was,
donating $108,000 for the future college educations
of ninety fifth graders at inner city San Antonio's
Gates Elementary School. "If you're going to tell a
kid that education is important," he declared at the
time, "then it's a lot stronger when you back it up."

□

While David's words and actions may have the most
selfless of motives, their effect has been to make him
even more desirable as a marketing personality.

Nike watched the developing Robinson phenomenon and realized that David might actually rival Michael as a shoe salesman. Their ad agency, Wieden &
Kennedy, saw him as a unique individual whose im-

age allowed them to combine commercial messages with public service announcements and humor. Nike's Fred Schreyer said, "David is such a positive role model he needs to make a statement." And they decided to build a major marketing campaign around him, as the chief spokesman for the Nike Force product line.

Thus was the fifteen-million-dollar "Mr. Robinson's Neighborhood" ad campaign born.

The campaign was conceived as a takeoff on the kids' TV classic, *Mister Rogers' Neighborhood.* It played up both the authoritative and gentle sides of David's nature, while at the same time making fun of its own suppositions.

In one remarkable 30-second spot, David co-starred with a diminutive, 79-year-old Czechoslovakian-born white-haired classical pianist, Rudolf Firkusny. After competing on the piano (playing a section of Chopin's "Polonaise Éroïque"), a humbled Mr. Robinson imperiously challenges the musician to some hoops. He slams and jams while the little old man stands impassively on the court, in his tuxedo. Finally Robinson calls a foul on the immobile Firkusny. The spot ends with David declaiming, "Geez, Mr. Firkusny's a better piano player than Mr. Robinson, but Mr. Robinson can really cream him at basketball."

David later called the Firkusny spot his favorite because the pianist's playing "was inspiring." And, recognizing the self-referential and mutually reinforcing nature of the advertising business, David faced the camera and tossed off the aside, "Bo may not know Diddley, but Mr. Robinson knows Beethoven."

Despite the overall positive response to the campaign, Nike still threw up a few air balls. The company tripped over its own feet trying to explain a spot in which David, after soothingly describing his technique for knotting and pumping his "special Nike shoes," asks the viewer, "Can you say, 'Kick some butt?'"

Before the ad premiered during the 1990 World Series, Nike spokeswoman Liz Dolan was certain that "everybody will get the joke." It didn't quite work out that way: Robinson was not happy with the placement of the commercial on prime time, thinking that the spot would be more appropriately aired only late at night; sectors of the public agreed.

There was criticism from other quarters as well. Earlier in the year, an article in *Sports Illustrated* deplored the high cost of premium basketball shoes. The piece pointed out that expensive sneakers had become status symbols among inner city gang members and that robberies had been committed for the shoes. It was the beginning of a campaign against the shoe companies.

In the ensuing uproar, Nike and Reebok were attacked for their pricing and marketing policies, which the critics claimed targeted poor black teens, and the celebrity endorsers (including David and Michael Jordan) were also criticized for participating in the campaign.

In response, Harvey Araton of the *New York Daily News* wrote, "My suggestion to anyone so ignorant to think some angry 15-year-old with a gun needs a one hundred thirty-five dollar sneaker as an excuse to hurt someone is to go ride the subway through Brooklyn at two A.M. with a pair of thirty dollar Converse and see what comes of that."

Araton also spoke with David to find out his feelings about the controversy and Robinson said, "These people are asking about problems that are bringing down entire communities, the breakdown of the family and loss of basic values. If they want to spend the time discussing why this is happening, I'd be glad to. I guarantee we won't be talking about sneakers."

Elsewhere, it was pointed out that the vast majority of hundred-dollar basketball shoes were not sold in inner cities, but to affluent white suburbanites. Nonetheless, the criticism continued unabated. Soon thereafter, Nike announced a five-million-dollar, proeducation, antidrug campaign starring Mr. Robinson and Michael, which, they explained, had been planned long before the controversy erupted.

Soon, 1,200 billboards across the country showed David holding a stack of books topped with a basketball. The bold message: "Don't be stoopid, stay in school."

And an antidrug spot was unveiled at the 1990 baseball All-Star Game. In it, David defined garbage as "anybody who's into drugs." With great conviction, he declared, "If you're into drugs, don't come into my neighborhood. Mr. Robinson doesn't like garbage in his neighborhood."

Ken Smikle, President of the African American Marketing and Media Association, objected to the Nike public service spots, "in which words like stupid and garbage are used to describe people in the target audience. We would never speak to ourselves like that," he said.

Liz Dolan, speaking for Nike, replied, "The [antidrug] ad is powerful because it's clear how David Robinson personally feels about how dangerous drugs are."

Another complaint about "Mr. Robinson's Neighborhood" came from NBC, which branded the campaign a rip-off of Eddie Murphy's scathing *Saturday Night Live* skits.

Despite the dissenting voices, "Mr. Robinson's Neighborhood" made David a household name. Even though he played basketball in the small San Antonio market (and the Spurs were rarely on national TV), he was suddenly in living rooms in New York, Chicago, Los Angeles, and every city, town, and suburb in between.

In many ways the campaign was remarkably effective. The spots were visually exciting, using quick cuts between the sedate, serious Mr. Robinson and the fast-paced action on the basketball court. And the sound, too, was unexpected and vivid.

But most effective of all was David himself. In reviewing the commercials, *Adweek* declared, "Mr. Robinson's acting throughout is quite good. The camera loves him; but the direction is unexpected enough to make him look cartoony. Seeing him shot from the ground up—all 85 inches of him—is terrifying enough; but at another point, a closeup on his newly shod foot reveals the true meaning of 'pedal extremity.' "

The true test of an ad, however, is how well it sells a product. And David sold sneakers. Jim Riswold, associate creative director of Wieden & Kennedy, said, "You know it [the campaign] works when people go into the stores and ask for the Mr. Robinson shoes."

□

By early 1991, many observers thought David could pitch in the same league as Michael Jordan, Bo Jackson, Magic Johnson, and Arnold Palmer. Although some thought that playing in a small south Texas city would hurt his marketability (Jordan was in Chicago, Johnson and Jackson in Los Angeles), others felt that the force of his personality was such that he transcended his distance from the nation's media centers.

He continued to perform for Nike, and a new series of spots released in the Spring of 1991 kept him in the public eye and reinforced his image as an intelligent, talented, and good-humored star. David was the subject of feature articles in *The New York Times,* in Canada's *MacLean's* magazine, and in *Adweek*—and found himself lionized on *Rolling Stone's* "hot list."

Matthew Grim, sports marketing columnist for *Adweek's Marketing Week,* said David was "at the cutting edge of a new generation of endorsers. He can act. He can play music. He is smart. He is an officer and a gentleman."

Pat Riley, who knew something about the spotlight as the flashy ex-Laker coach, NBC commentator, and soon-to-be New York Knick coach, remarked: "Magic Johnson and Michael Jordan are the only rock stars to play basketball. Those guys are part of a cult that has an international following. I think

David can command that. Whether or not he wants
to will be determined on how he embraces that life-
style."

In a remarkably short period of time, David had
become a full-scale celebrity. He still valued his privacy, but as he looked ahead to his future, he knew
there was no turning back.

In the summer of 1991, after Michael Jordan left
Coke to sign a multiyear deal with Gatorade, David
stepped up to sign another lucrative deal, to promote
Coca-Cola Classic.

Mr. Robinson was becoming as much a force in
the marketplace as he was on the basketball court. As
Rick Welts, president of NBA Properties, said: "We
agree with the prediction Pat Riley made recently on
NBC that the 1990s will be his decade."

EPILOGUE

SHOOTING
FOR THE TOP

How high is up for David Robinson? Most basketball observers have not yet discovered a limit, predicting only that he will be the best center of the nineties, and in all likelihood one of the best in history.

Like most great players, David places more value on winning than on individual stats. He is aware that Michael Jordan didn't win a title until his seventh year in the league, and that Patrick Ewing offered to turn his back on more than thirty million dollars rather than play out the rest of his career on a losing team. Robinson knows that Magic and Bird and Isiah, despite their brilliant individual accomplishments, are measured more by the championships they've won than by their records. And he also knows that in an earlier era, when Bill Russell's success was predicated on the Celtic dynasty which he led, Wilt Chamberlain, despite being a four-time MVP and the holder of numerous All-Time NBA records, was looked on in some quarters as unfulfilled because he captured only two championships.

Already entrenched as one of the league's super-stars, San Antonio's Number 50 knows that the only way he can fulfill his promise is by bringing a championship to his team. Last season's playoff loss to the Warriors still hurts, and the disappointment has motivated him to become more focused than ever on winning.

Thus David is still working on improving his game, trying to go beyond his limitations and build himself up, both physically and spiritually, for a run at the title.

In an effort to get closer to the ultimate goal, he was tutored in the summer of '91 by the Boston Celtics' great Dave Cowens, one of the quickest, most mobile centers ever. Cowens worked with him to develop the go-to post move he lacks.

David is a force to be reckoned with in the NBA, both on the court and off. He was the elixir that revived a dying franchise, and the importance of the young superstar—to both the Spurs and the league—is incontrovertible. Michael is at his prime, Bird past his, and Magic is gone. Of all the top draws in the league, David is the youngest. He is the league's future, and he knows it.

David, then, has a lot more power with management than the average star in the most player-oriented league in pro sports. He can talk to them about personnel decisions—and they have to listen. And when he asked Larry Brown last summer not to leave the Spurs for college coaching, the coach did not ignore his wishes.

□

Whatever the Spurs do this playoff season, David Robinson will be playing basketball in the summer of '92. As John Thompson predicted after the 1988 Olympics, NBA stars are now allowed to play in the games. And that decision gives David a second chance to go for the gold.

Unlike the disaster in Seoul, in Barcelona the United States will have more than just one big man to rely on. The American team, coached by Chuck Daly —and including Michael Jordan, Larry Bird, Karl Malone, Patrick Ewing, Scottie Pippin, John Stockton, Charles Barkley, and Chris Mullin—won't be satisfied with the silver.

Nor will David ever be content with coming in second—in the Olympics or anywhere else.

APPENDIX

THE CAREER STATS

DAVID ROBINSON'S NAVAL ACADEMY RECORDS

1.	Career points	2,669
2.	Points in a season	903
3.	Points in a game	50
4.	Scoring average, season	28.2
5.	Double-figure games, career	98
6.	Double-figures games, season	35
7.	Consecutive double-figure games	67
8.	30-point games, career	30
9.	30-point games, season	15
10.	Consecutive 30-point games	3
11.	Rebounds, career	1,314
12.	Rebounds, season	455
13.	Rebounds, game	25
14.	Blocked shots, career	516*
15.	Blocked shots, season	207*
16.	Blocked shots, game	14*
17.	Field goals made, career	1,032
18.	Field goals made, season	350
19.	Field goals made, game	22
20.	Field goal attempts, career	1,683
21.	Field goal attempts, game	40
22.	Field goal percentage, career	.613
23.	Field goal percentage, season	.644
24.	Field goal percentage, game	1.000
25.	Free throws made, career	604
26.	Free throws made, season	208
27.	Free throws made, game	21
28.	Free throw attempts, career	964
29.	Free throw attempts, season	331
30.	Free throw attempts, game	27
31.	Free throw percentage, game	1.000
32.	Steals, career	160
33.	Steals, season	66

* NCAA record.

DAVID ROBINSON'S CAREER RECORDS

College Stats (at the U.S. Naval Academy)

Totals

Year	Games/Starts	FG/FGA	Pct.	FT/FTA	Pct.	Reb.	RebPG	A	APG	BLK	BPG	TP	PPG
1983–1984	28/0	86/138	.623	42/73	.575	111	4.0	6	0.2	37	1.3	214	7.6
1984–1985	32/32	302/469	.644	152/243	.626	370	11.6	19	0.6	128	4.0	756	23.6
1985–1986	35/35	294/484	.607	208/331	.628	455	13.0	24	0.7	207	5.9	796	22.7
1986–1987	32/32	350/592	.591	202/317	.617	378	11.8	33	1.0	144	4.5	903	28.2
TOTALS	127/99	1032/1683	.613	604/964	.627	1314	10.3	82	0.6	516	4.1	2669	21.0

NCAA Tournament

Year	Games	Min.	FG/FGA	Pct.	FT/FTA	Pct.	Reb.	RebPG	A	APG	TO	PF/DQ	S	BLK	BPG	TP	PPG
1985	2	76	19/32	.594	2/10	.200	26	13.0	0	0.0	5	4/0	2	5	2.5	40	20.0
1986	4	144	35/57	.614	40/55	.727	47	11.8	3	0.7	12	14/1	7	23	5.8	110	27.8
1987	1	40	22/37	.595	6/12	.500	13	13.0	0	0.0	1	2/0	3	2	2.0	50	50.0
TOTALS	7	260	76/126	.603	48/77	.623	86	12.3	3	0.4	18	20/1	12	30	4.2	200	28.6

Professional Stats (with the San Antonio Spurs)

Regular Season

Year	Games	Min.	2 Pt. FG/FGA	Pct.	3 Pt. FG/FGA	Pct.	FT/FTA	Pct.
1989–1990	82	3002	690/1300	.531	0/2	.000	613/837	.732
1990–1991	82	3095	754/1366	.552	1/7	.143	592/777	.762
2 YEARS	164	6097	1444/2666	.542	1/9	.111	1205/1614	.747

Year	Reb. O/T	RebPG	A	APG	TO	PF/DQ	S	BLK	BPG	TP	PPG
1989–1990	303/983	12.0	164	2.0	138	259/3	257	319	3.9	1993	24.3
1990–1991	335/1063	13.0	208	2.5	270	264/5	127	320	3.9	2101	25.6
2 YEARS	638/2046	12.5	372	2.3	408	523/8	385	639	3.9	4094	25.0

Playoffs

| | | | 2 Pt. | | 3 Pt. | | | |
Year	Games	Min.	FG/FGA	Pct.	FG/FGA	Pct.	FT/FTA	Pct.
1990	10	375	89/167	.533	0/0	—	65/96	.677
1991	4	166	35/51	.686	0/1	.000	33/38	.868
2 YEARS	14	541	124/218	.569	0/1	.000	98/134	.731

Year	Reb. O/T	RebPG	A	APG	TO	PF/DQ	S	BLK	BPG	TP	PPG
1990	36/120	12.0	23	2.3	24	35/1	11	40	4.0	243	24.3
1991	11/54	13.5	8	2.0	15	11/0	6	15	3.8	103	25.8
2 YEARS	47/174	12.4	31	2.2	39	46/1	17	55	3.9	346	24.7